The Swan's Palette

The Swan's Palette

a collection
of recipes from the

**Forward Arts Foundation
of Atlanta**

ABOUT OUR ARTIST

Our cover art was created by Rosie Clark, a native Atlantan well known for her spectacular works. Her medium is scratchboard and acrylic, where she combines her whimsical personality with her artistic talent in depicting animals and vegetables. She has been a longtime good friend of the Forward Arts Foundation and has donated her talent to this book. We are very grateful to her. Rosie's paintings can be seen and purchased at the Swan Coach House Gift Shop.

The Swan's Palette

A collection of recipes from
the Forward Arts Foundation

Copyright © 2000
Forward Arts Foundation
3130 Slaton Drive, Northwest
Atlanta, Georgia 30305

Library of Congress Number: 00-133053
ISBN: 978-0967953700

Designed, Edited, and Manufactured by
Favorite Recipes® Press
An imprint of

P.O. Box 305142
Nashville, Tennessee 37230
1-800-358-0560

Book Design: Jim Scott
Art Director: Steve Newman
Project Manager: Nicki Pendleton Wood

Manufactured in China
First Printing 2000: 12,500 copies
Second Printing 2001: 12,500 copies
Third Printing 2015: 1,000 copies

CONTENTS

On the grounds of the Atlanta History Center,
the Swan Coach House reflects Atlanta's
tradition of gracious hospitality. Once the carriage house of the historic
Swan House, today the Swan Coach House is a restaurant, gift shop, and art gallery
managed by the Forward Arts Foundation, a nonprofit organization which
promotes the visual arts in Atlanta, Georgia.

FORWARD ARTS FOUNDATION
3130 Slaton Drive, Northwest
Atlanta, Georgia 30305

Telephone: 404-261-9855
www.swancoachhouse.com

FORWARD ARTS FOUNDATION

In 1965, a group of extraordinary women established the Forward Arts Foundation in Atlanta, Georgia. Their steadfast mission to promote and support the visual arts in metro Atlanta continues to this day. These distinguished arts patrons, whose dynamic leadership was matched by their determination, transformed the carriage house of the Swan House estate into a restaurant, gift shop and, in 1984, an art gallery. Throughout its history, the Forward Arts Foundation has raised significant funds in support of the visual arts and has created an indelible mark on Atlanta's arts landscape.

THE RESTAURANT

Featuring the best of the New South, the Swan Coach House Restaurant is a full service, "white tablecloth" restaurant and well-established venue for meetings, parties and special events. The restaurant serves sophisticated regional fare with Southern favorites such as cheese straws, secret-recipe chicken salad and frozen fruit salad. Lunch is served Monday through Saturday. No reservations are necessary and valet parking is available at the entrance.

THE GIFT SHOP

This signature boutique features unique clothing, home accessories, tableware, statement jewelry and children's items. Wedding, bridal, graduation and baby gifts from the Swan Coach House Gift Shop are an Atlanta tradition. The shop also hosts book signings, trunk shows and other events throughout the year.

THE ART GALLERY

Completed in 1984, the Swan Coach House Gallery is an expansion of the original Swan Coach House footprint and has won rave reviews for its design and exhibitions. Notably, the gallery hosts an annual series of special exhibitions that include various types of artistic expressions from nationally and internationally renowned artists. In the past decade, the gallery turned its focus to featuring and promoting works by Southern artists, and started the Emerging Artist Award program.

On its thirtieth anniversary in 1995, the Forward Arts Foundation was hailed by the director of the High Museum of Art in Atlanta, Georgia, for its unique contributions. "No organization promoting the visual arts has achieved such spectacular results over the past thirty years as the Forward Arts Foundation."

Acquisitions made possible by the Foundation for the High Museum of Art include Claude Monet's *Autumn on the Seine, Argenteuil*; Frederic Bazille's *The Beach at Sainte-Adresse*; Camille Pissarro's *Bouquet of Flowers*; and *Ravine in the Morvan, near Lormes* by Camille Corot. The acclaimed exhibitions "Degas and America: The Early Collectors;" "Henri Matisse: Masterworks from The Museum of Modern Art;" and a spectacular Picasso presentation also were made possible through lead gifts by the Foundation.

Financial gifts by the Foundation to the Atlanta History Center have enabled the acquisition of the entrance gates to Swan House and many decorative art items, including the Swan Tables in the dining room. A 1999 grant helped insure the restoration of this circa 1920 Italianate villa. The colonnade entrance of the Atlanta History Museum as well as the orientation video also were given by the Foundation.

The Foundation's "Emerging Artist Award" has supported individual artists in the metro Atlanta area since 2000. Presented annually, this coveted award provides a monetary grant and solo exhibition to an outstanding artist, chosen by an expert panel of arts professionals.

In addition to the High Museum of Art and Atlanta History Center, the Forward Arts Foundation has provided significant support for the Michael C. Carlos Museum, MOCA GA, the Georgia Museum of Art, the Atlanta Contemporary Arts Center, the Atlanta Botanical Garden, the Atlanta Beltline, the Cherokee Garden Library, Burnaway and others. The Foundation remains steadfastly committed to focused community grant making.

DEDICATION

Today, Forward Arts Foundation members celebrate over 50 years of service. They continue the hands-on tradition of the founding members, energetically managing the Swan Coach House and focusing on creating additional funds for the visual arts in Atlanta.

This cookbook's title, *The Swan's Palette,* jointly reflects the Foundation's mission of volunteer support for the visual arts and of its beginning as a charming tearoom.

The Swan's Palette is dedicated to the fourteen legendary Atlanta ladies who established the Forward Arts Foundation.

COOKBOOK COMMITTEE

CO-CHAIRS

Wesley Moran

Betsy West

RECIPE CO-CHAIRS

Nancy Lynn

Laura Spearman

ART DESIGN

Peaches Page

COMMITTEE-AT-LARGE

Robyn Barkin

Laura Blackburn

Nancy Caswell

Peggy Clinkscales

Elizabeth Hale

Wynn Henderson

Wanda Hopkins

Robin Howell

Cappy Livezey

Mary Mobley

Jean Nunnally

Jill Nunnally

Eleanor Ratchford

Harriet Shaffer

Susan Tucker

Becky Warner

Joan White

Kathy York

MENUS

Mexican Fiesta Teen Party

Roasted Garlic Nachos

Mexican Hat Dance with Tortilla Chips

*Grilled Shrimp with Black Bean
and Mango Salsa*

Chicken Tortilla Casserole

Whole Kernel Corn Bread

Lemon Curd Tartlets

....

Forward Arts Foundation Luncheon

Spiced Pecans

Salmon Mousse with Cucumber Sauce

Swan Coach House Strawberry Soup

*Chicken Florentine with
Sherry Artichoke Sauce*

Pumpkin Muffins

Lemon Ice Cream with Raspberry Sauce

....

Summer Luau

Cocktail Pork Loin with Homemade Rolls

Thai Crab Dip with Crudités

Vidalia Onion Spread

Curried Chicken Salad

Chinese Slaw

Piña Colada Cake

Elegant Dinner Party

Crab Meat Mornay with Crackers

Zesty Tomato Tartlets

Smoked Salmon Pinwheels

Gingered Carrot Vichyssoise

Cornucopia Salad

*Pork Tenderloin with
Balsamic Raisin Sauce*

Scalloped Potatoes with Truffle Crema

Southern Dinner Rolls

Bananas Foster

....

Christmas Eve Dinner

Caviar Pie

Bleu Cheese Puffs

*Mixed Greens with
Sugared Walnuts and
Balsamic Vinaigrette*

*Beef Stew with Fennel
and Pecans*

Buttery Biscuit Rolls

*Pumpkin Chiffon Pie
or Old-Fashioned Fig Cake*

MENUS

Easter Lunch

Mushroom Croustades

Hot Spinach Salad

Mint-Barbecued Leg of Lamb

*Noodles with Smoked Salmon and
Dill Sauce*

*Swan Coach House Asparagus
with Orange Basil Hollandaise*

Mom's Best Biscuits

Blueberry Crisp

Dinner at Chastain Park

Gazpacho

London Broil with Pineapple Salsa

*Tortellini with Sun-Dried
Tomatoes and Pepperoni*

Snow Pea Salad

Buttermilk Pound Cake with Fresh Fruit

Summer Alfresco Dinner

Roquefort Gougères

Cold and Spicy Moroccan Tomato Soup

Veal Giardino

Nutted Wild Rice

Southern Dinner Rolls

Summer Fruit Tart

Fourth-of-July Lake Party

Lake Burton Dip with Potato Chips

Pickled Shrimp

Oven-Glazed Spareribs

Lemon Slaw

Mean Baked Beans

Broccoli Corn Bread

Fresh Apple Cake

Sparkling Cocktail Party

*Sun-Dried Tomato and
Provolone Bread with Champagne Mustard
and Smoked Turkey*

Vegetable Spread

Shrimp Mold

Cranberry-Glazed Brie

Curry Dip with Vegetables

Hot and Tangy Meatballs

*Warm Bleu Cheese Dip with
Garlic and Bacon*

Assorted Breads, Crackers and Chips

Lemon Curd Tartlets

*Chocolate Sherry
Cream Bars*

Beverages and Starters

Fizzy Three-Fruit Drink

2 cups chilled orange juice,
  preferably fresh
1 cup chilled cranberry juice
  cocktail
1 cup chilled sparkling white
  grape juice

- MIX THE ORANGE juice and cranberry juice cocktail in a pitcher. Chill until ready to serve. Add the sparkling white grape juice just before serving.

Plantation Cooler

3 (12-ounce) cans frozen
  lemonade concentrate
3 (12-ounce) cans frozen
  orange juice concentrate
3 (46-ounce) cans
  pineapple juice
3 quarts ginger ale, chilled
2 quarts club soda, chilled
1 quart tonic water, chilled
1 gallon ice water
1 or 2 ice ring molds

- COMBINE THE LEMONADE concentrate, orange juice concentrate, pineapple juice, ginger ale, club soda, tonic water and ice water in a large punch bowl and mix well.

- Float the ice molds in the punch just before serving.

For **Sugar-Free Tea Punch,** combine ½ cup plus 2 teaspoons iced tea mix with artificial sweetener and lemon extract, 2 cups orange juice and ⅓ to ½ cup lemon juice in a 1-gallon pitcher. Add enough water to make about a gallon, tasting the mixture as you add the water. You may not need all the water. Makes 1 gallon.

Rich Eggnog

MAKES ABOUT 22 (½-CUP) SERVINGS

12 egg yolks
2 cups sugar
26 ounces (a fifth) bourbon
   whiskey
12 egg whites
1 quart whipping cream

- BEAT THE EGG yolks in a bowl until pale yellow. Beat in the sugar gradually. Beat in the bourbon gradually. Beat the egg whites in a bowl with an electric mixer until stiff peaks form.

- Beat the whipping cream in a chilled bowl until stiff peaks form. Fold the egg whites and cream into the egg yolk mixture. Refrigerate, covered, until ready to serve. Prepare eggnog no more than 1 hour in advance.

Hot Holiday Cider

MAKES 16 (½-CUP) SERVINGS

4 cups apple juice
4 cups cranberry juice
   cocktail
1 (6-ounce) can frozen
   lemonade concentrate
3/4 cup packed brown sugar
1 teaspoon cinnamon

- COMBINE THE APPLE juice, cranberry juice cocktail, lemonade concentrate, brown sugar and cinnamon in a saucepan and mix well. Heat over low heat until the sugar dissolves, stirring occasionally. Serve hot.

French Hot Chocolate

4 ounces semisweet
   chocolate
1/4 cup light corn syrup
1/2 teaspoon vanilla extract
4 cups milk
1 cup whipping cream,
   whipped
8 peppermint sticks

- MELT THE CHOCOLATE with the corn syrup in the top of a double boiler over simmering water. Refrigerate, covered, for 30 minutes. Add the vanilla and mix well. Heat the milk in a saucepan until bubbles form around the edges. Add the chocolate mixture and mix well.

- Divide the whipped cream among 8 mugs. Pour the chocolate mixture over the whipped cream. Garnish with a peppermint stick.

Hot Tomato Sip

1 (10-ounce) can tomato
   soup
1 (10-ounce) can beef broth
10 ounces pale golden
   sherry

- COMBINE THE TOMATO soup, beef broth and sherry in a saucepan and mix well. Heat over low heat until warm. Serve warm in mugs.

Sparkling Iced Tea

MAKES ABOUT 12 (1-CUP) SERVINGS

2 quarts strong hot tea
6 large mint sprigs
Sugar to taste
1 quart ginger ale
Fresh mint leaves

- POUR THE HOT tea over the mint sprigs in a large pitcher. Let steep for 10 minutes. Remove the mint sprigs. Add sugar to taste and mix well. Let cool until ready to serve. Stir in the ginger ale. Pour over ice in glasses and garnish with mint leaves just before serving.

Bleu Cheese Puffs

MAKES 48 SERVINGS

16 ounces cream cheese, softened
1 cup mayonnaise
1 tablespoon minced onion
1/4 cup minced fresh chives
3 to 4 ounces bleu cheese, crumbled
1/2 teaspoon cayenne pepper
2 loaves thin-sliced firm white bread
Paprika for garnish

- COMBINE THE CREAM cheese and mayonnaise in a medium bowl and mix well. Stir in the onion, chives, bleu cheese and cayenne pepper. Cut the bread into rounds with a 1 1/2-inch to 2-inch round cutter. Spread 1 tablespoon of the cheese mixture on each round.

- Place the rounds on a baking sheet. Freeze, covered, until firm. When ready to serve, bake the rounds on the baking sheet in a 350-degree oven for 15 minutes. Sprinkle with paprika. Serve immediately.

- NOTE: You may transfer the frozen rounds to plastic bags for longer freezer storage.

Roquefort Gougères

1 cup milk
1/2 cup (1 stick) unsalted
  butter
1 teaspoon salt
1 cup sifted unbleached
  flour
4 eggs
1 1/2 cups crumbled
  Roquefort cheese
1 egg
2 tablespoons freshly grated
  Parmesan cheese

- COMBINE THE MILK, butter and salt in a small saucepan. Bring to a boil. Remove from the heat. Add the flour. Beat mixture vigorously. Return the saucepan to medium heat and cook until the mixture pulls away from the sides of the pan, stirring constantly.

- Remove the pan from the heat. Add the 4 eggs, 1 at a time, beating well after each addition. Stir in the Roquefort cheese. Drop the batter by tablespoonfuls onto a greased baking sheet. Beat the egg in a small bowl. Brush beaten egg over each puff; sprinkle with the Parmesan cheese.

- Bake on the center oven rack at 375 degrees for 10 minutes. Reduce the oven temperature to 350 degrees. Bake about 5 to 10 minutes longer or until well browned.

- NOTE: Baked gougères may be frozen, then reheated.

Cranberry-Glazed Brie

3 cups cranberries
3/4 cup packed light brown
   sugar
1/3 cup dried currants
1/3 cup water
1/8 teaspoon dry mustard
1/8 teaspoon allspice
1/8 teaspoon cardamom
1/8 teaspoon ground cloves
1/8 teaspoon ground ginger
1 (2-pound) Brie cheese

- COMBINE THE CRANBERRIES, brown sugar, currants, water, dry mustard, allspice, cardamom, cloves and ginger in a large nonaluminum saucepan and mix well.

- Cook over medium heat for 5 minutes or until nearly all the cranberries pop, stirring frequently. Let cool to room temperature.

- Cut a circle in the top of the cheese through the rind, leaving a 1/2-inch border and taking care not to cut through the sides of the cheese. Remove the circle of rind carefully. Place the cheese on a baking sheet lined with foil. Spread the cranberry mixture over the cheese.

- Bake at 300 degrees for 12 to 15 minutes or until soft. Place on a serving plate. Serve with ginger thins and other crackers.

Cheese Quesadillas

MAKES 30 SERVINGS

1/2 cup (1 stick) butter,
  softened
1 pound Monterey Jack
  cheese, shredded
Green and white parts of
  8 green onions,
  thinly sliced
1/2 cup drained chopped
  pimentos
4 pickled jalapeños, seeded,
  minced
3 tablespoons chopped
  cilantro, or 1/2 teaspoon
  ground coriander
1 teaspoon ground cumin
5 (10-inch) or 8 (7-inch)
  flour tortillas

- COMBINE THE BUTTER, cheese, green onions, pimentos, jalapeños, cilantro and cumin in a bowl and mix well.

- Prick the tortillas in several places with a fork to prevent puffing and place on a baking sheet. Toast the tortillas in a 400-degree oven for 2 to 3 minutes or until light brown.

- Spread a scant 1/4 cup of the cheese mixture on each tortilla. Bake at 400 degrees for 2 to 3 minutes. Cut into wedges with a rolling pizza cutter.

- NOTE: You may also grill the quesadillas on a grill griddle over hot coals; close the lid when grilling.

Lemon Chicken Bites

MAKES 12 SERVINGS

1 pound boneless chicken,
   cut into thin strips
1 egg, lightly beaten
2 drops of sesame oil
1 tablespoon cornstarch
Salt and pepper to taste
Peanut oil
$1/2$ cup water
2 tablespoons white wine
   vinegar
2 tablespoons lemon juice
$1/3$ cup sugar
2 drops of lemon extract
1 drop of sesame oil
1 tablespoon cornstarch
1 tablespoon water

- COMBINE THE CHICKEN, egg, 2 drops of sesame oil, 1 tablespoon cornstarch, salt and pepper in a bowl and mix well.

- Deep-fry the chicken in 375-degree peanut oil until brown. Drain on paper towels and cut into bite-size pieces. Keep warm.

- Combine $1/2$ cup water, vinegar, lemon juice, sugar, lemon extract, 1 drop of sesame oil and salt in a small saucepan. Bring to a boil over medium-high heat.

- Combine 1 tablespoon cornstarch with 1 tablespoon water in a small bowl and mix well. Stir into the lemon juice mixture. Cook until smooth and clear, stirring constantly. Add the chicken and mix well. Spoon into a chafing dish. Serve with wooden picks.

Ham and Swiss Cheese Party Sandwiches

MAKES 48 SERVINGS

1 cup (2 sticks) butter
4 ounces Dijon mustard
2 tablespoons poppy seeds
2 (24-count) packages
   party rolls
1½ pounds Swiss cheese,
   sliced into small squares
1 pound thinly-sliced deli
   ham, cut into small
   squares

- MELT THE BUTTER in a small saucepan over low heat or microwave in a microwave-safe bowl until melted. Add the mustard and poppy seeds and mix well. Slice the rolls into halves horizontally.

- Spread the butter mixture over the bottom half. Top with a slice of cheese, then a slice of ham. Top with upper half of rolls. Arrange the sandwiches on a baking sheet with sides. Bake at 350 degrees for 8 minutes or until the cheese is melted.

Spiced Pecans

MAKES 4 CUPS

1 egg white, lightly beaten
2 tablespoons cold water
½ cup sugar
¼ teaspoon ground cloves
¼ teaspoon allspice
¼ teaspoon cinnamon
½ teaspoon salt
4 cups pecan halves

- COMBINE THE EGG white, cold water, sugar, cloves, allspice, cinnamon and salt in a large bowl and mix well. Let stand for 15 minutes. Add the pecan halves and mix well.

- Spread the mixture evenly over 2 greased baking sheets. Bake at 250 degrees for 1 hour. Loosen pecans from sheets immediately. Let cool. Store in an airtight container.

Cocktail Pork Loin

MAKES ABOUT 48 SERVINGS

6 pounds pork loin roast
Thyme to taste
Dry mustard to taste
$1/2$ cup dry sherry
$1/2$ cup soy sauce
2 tablespoons ground ginger
3 garlic cloves, crushed
8 ounces currant or
    apple jelly
1 tablespoon soy sauce
2 tablespoons dry sherry
Pepper jelly
Homemade rolls

- RUB THE ROAST all over with thyme and dry mustard. Combine the $1/2$ cup sherry, $1/2$ cup soy sauce, ginger and garlic in a large bowl and mix well. Add the pork and turn to coat with the mixture. Refrigerate, covered, for at least 8 hours. Remove the pork from the marinade, reserving the marinade. Pour the reserved marinade into a saucepan. Bring to a boil, stirring frequently. Remove from the heat.

- Bake the pork at 325 degrees for 25 minutes per pound, basting often with the reserved marinade.

- Melt the currant or apple jelly in a saucepan over medium heat. Add the 1 tablespoon soy sauce and 2 tablespoons sherry and mix well. Let stand until cool.

- Place the roast on a rack over a shallow pan. Spoon the jelly glaze over the pork repeatedly until it is thickly and evenly glazed. Slice and serve with pepper jelly and homemade rolls.

Smoked Salmon Pinwheels

8 ounces cream cheese, softened
2 teaspoons fresh lemon juice
1/2 teaspoon grated onion (optional)
1/8 teaspoon freshly ground pepper
4 (7-inch) flour tortillas
4 teaspoons drained nonpareil-size capers
1/2 pound thinly sliced smoked salmon
Dill sprigs

- COMBINE THE CREAM cheese, lemon juice, onion and pepper in a bowl and mix well. Spread evenly over the tortillas. Sprinkle the capers over the cream cheese. Add a layer of smoked salmon. Roll each tortilla tightly.

- Chill, covered, in the refrigerator until firm. Slice each roll into 6 pinwheels when ready to serve. Garnish each pinwheel with a sprig of dill.

Pickled Shrimp

1 quart shrimp, cooked, peeled, deveined
2 cups sliced onions
1 (2-ounce) bottle capers
1/3 cup fresh lemon juice
2 teaspoons salt
Dash of Tabasco sauce
1 teaspoon sugar
1 cup vegetable oil
1 cup vinegar
3/4 cup water
2 bay leaves
2 1/2 teaspoons celery seeds

- LAYER THE SHRIMP, onions and capers alternately in 1 or more large jars. Combine the lemon juice, salt, Tabasco sauce, sugar, oil, vinegar, water, bay leaves and celery seeds in a bowl and mix well.

- Pour over the shrimp mixture. Cover the jar and refrigerate for at least 8 hours before serving.

Hot and Tangy Meatballs

MAKES 36 SERVINGS

Tangy Sauce

3/4 cup ketchup
1/2 cup water
1/4 cup cider vinegar
2 tablespoons brown sugar
1 tablespoon minced onion
2 teaspoons Worcestershire
  sauce
1 1/2 teaspoons salt
1 teaspoon dry mustard
3 drops of hot pepper sauce
Pinch of cayenne pepper

Meatballs

1 pound ground beef
1 cup fine bread crumbs
1 3/4 tablespoons minced
  onion
3/4 teaspoon horseradish
3 drops of hot pepper sauce
2 eggs, beaten
1 teaspoon salt
3/4 teaspoon pepper
3/4 teaspoon MSG
1 tablespoon butter

- FOR THE SAUCE, combine the ketchup, water, vinegar, brown sugar, onion, Worcestershire sauce, salt, mustard, hot pepper sauce and cayenne pepper in a bowl and mix well.

- For the meatballs, combine the beef, bread crumbs, onion, horseradish, hot pepper sauce and eggs in a bowl and mix well. Season with the salt, pepper and MSG. Roll the beef mixture into 3/4-inch balls. Melt the butter in a skillet. Add the meatballs and brown, stirring or shaking the skillet frequently; drain.

- To assemble, pour the sauce over the meatballs. Cook, covered, for 10 minutes, shaking or stirring occasionally. Keep warm over a pan of simmering water.

- NOTE: The cooked meatballs may be frozen and reheated when ready to serve.

Roasted Garlic Nachos

2 large heads garlic,
    separated into cloves
    and peeled
2 tablespoons vegetable oil
Tortilla chips
$1/4$ cup chopped red onion
1 (4-ounce) can chopped
    green chiles, drained
$1/3$ cup sliced pimento-
    stuffed green olives
$1^1/2$ cups shredded pepper
    Jack cheese
Chopped cilantro and green
    onion tops

- COAT THE GARLIC with the oil. Roast at 375 degrees on a baking sheet for 30 minutes or until soft and golden brown. Cover a 9x13-inch baking pan with foil. Arrange a layer of tortilla chips in the prepared pan. Mash the garlic and mix with the onion, green chiles and olives in a bowl. Spread evenly over the chips. Top with the cheese.

- Bake at 400 degrees for 5 minutes or until the cheese melts. Garnish with cilantro and green onion.

Tortilla Roll-Ups

8 ounces cream cheese,
    softened
1 (4-ounce) can chopped
    black olives, drained
1 (4-ounce) can chopped
    green chiles, drained
1 teaspoon (or more)
    picante sauce
1 (10-count) package large
    flour tortillas

- BEAT THE CREAM cheese, black olives, green chiles and picante sauce in a bowl and mix well.

- Spread a heaping tablespoon of the mixture evenly over each tortilla. Roll up the tortillas as for a jelly roll. Slice into 1-inch pieces. Secure the slices with wooden picks.

Mushroom Croustades

2 tablespoons butter,
  softened
24 thin slices white bread
3 tablespoons minced
  shallots
1/4 cup (1/2 stick) butter
8 ounces mushrooms,
  finely chopped
2 tablespoons flour
1 cup heavy cream
1 1/2 tablespoons minced
  chives
1 tablespoon minced parsley
1/2 teaspoon lemon juice
1/2 teaspoon salt
1/8 teaspoon cayenne
  pepper
2 tablespoons grated
  Parmesan cheese
2 tablespoons minced
  parsley
Butter

- COAT MINIATURE MUFFIN cups heavily with the 2 tablespoons butter. Cut a 3-inch round from each slice of bread with a biscuit cutter. Press into the prepared pans to form cups. Bake at 400 degrees for 10 minutes. Let cool in tins for 2 minutes. Remove and cool completely.

- Sauté the shallots in the 1/4 cup butter in a heavy skillet for 1 minute. Add the mushrooms. Simmer for about 10 minutes or until all the liquid has evaporated. Remove the skillet from the heat and stir in the flour.

- Pour the cream into the skillet. Cook over medium-high heat until mixtures comes to a boil and thickens, stirring constantly. Remove from the heat. Add the chives, 1 tablespoon parsley, lemon juice, salt and cayenne pepper and mix well. Let cool and refrigerate, covered, until ready to fill the toast shells.

- Spoon the mushroom mixture into the toast shells. Sprinkle with the Parmesan cheese and 2 tablespoons parsley. Dot with butter. Arrange on an ungreased baking sheet. Bake at 350 degrees for 10 minutes. Turn the oven temperature to broil; brown croustades. Serve immediately.

- NOTE: You may freeze the croustades after filling but before sprinkling with Parmesan and parsley. Freeze on a baking sheet, then pack into plastic bags. Thaw before baking, then proceed as the recipe directs.

Tomato Devils

For **Quick Little Pizzas,** top small prebaked pizza shells with purchased marinara sauce or pesto. Sprinkle with your favorite cheese, then a few chopped fresh herbs, or layer with meats and vegetables. A tasty combination is marinara sauce topped with Brie cheese and fresh basil. Or try pesto with Italian fontina cheese and a little roasted garlic.

24 small bread rounds or cocktail rye slices
1 cup shredded Cheddar, Jarlsberg or Monterey Jack cheese
2 bunches green onions, thinly sliced
$1/2$ green bell pepper, finely chopped
$2/3$ cup mayonnaise
$1/2$ teaspoon garlic salt
$1/8$ teaspoon cayenne pepper
$1/3$ cup mayonnaise
1 pint baby yellow or cherry tomatoes, sliced
8 bacon slices, cooked and crumbled

- TOAST ONE SIDE of each bread round under a broiler. Cover the bread with foil and set aside.

- Combine the cheese, green onions, bell pepper and $2/3$ cup mayonnaise in a large bowl and mix well. Season with the garlic salt and cayenne pepper.

- Spread the untoasted sides of the bread rounds with the $1/3$ cup mayonnaise. Place on a baking sheet. Top with the tomato slices. Spread with the cheese mixture. Sprinkle with the bacon. Bake at 350 degrees until bubbly and brown. Serve immediately.

- NOTE: You may also use regular size tomatoes and cut larger bread rounds.

Zesty Tomato Tartlets

MAKES **20** SERVINGS

5 or 6 medium tomatoes,
   peeled, seeded, chopped
2 deep-dish refrigerated
   pie pastries
Jane's Krazy Mixed-up Salt
   to taste
1 cup mayonnaise
1 cup grated Parmesan
   cheese
$1/2$ teaspoon garlic powder
20 round butter crackers,
   crushed

- PLACE THE TOMATOES in a colander and let stand to drain for 30 minutes. Bring the pie pastries to room temperature. Cut into rounds with a 2-inch biscuit cutter. Press the pastry into miniature muffin cups. Prick bottom of pastries with a fork.

- Bake at 350 degrees 10 minutes or until golden brown. Let cool. You may freeze the tartlet shells at this point, then thaw and fill when ready to use.

- Fill the shells with the drained tomatoes and sprinkle with the salt. Combine the mayonnaise, Parmesan cheese and garlic powder in a bowl and mix well. Spoon enough of the mixture over the tomatoes to cover them. Sprinkle with the cracker crumbs. Bake at 350 degrees for 15 to 20 minutes.

Tomato and Goat Cheese Appetizer

Large ripe tomatoes
Salt to taste
Fresh whole basil leaves
Goat cheese

- CUT THE TOMATOES into thick slices. Arrange on a large heavy greased baking sheet or in a greased rectangular baking dish. Sprinkle with salt. Place a fresh basil leaf on each tomato slice. Top with a heaping spoonful of the goat cheese.

- Broil the tomatoes until the cheese begins to melt and forms a golden brown crust. Serve hot on individual plates with a bed of Bibb or Boston lettuce if desired.

Marinated Tomatoes and Brie

1 pound Brie cheese
4 large ripe tomatoes,
    seeded and cut into
    1/2-inch cubes
1 cup fresh basil leaves,
    cut into strips
3 garlic cloves, finely
    minced
2/3 cup extra-virgin olive oil
1 teaspoon salt
1/2 teaspoon freshly ground
    pepper

- CUT THE RIND off the cheese. Cut the cheese into irregular small pieces. Combine with the tomatoes, basil, garlic, olive oil, salt and pepper in a serving bowl and mix well.

- Let stand, covered, at room temperature for at least 2 hours. Serve as a spread with crusty French bread.

Warm Bleu Cheese Dip with Garlic and Bacon

MAKES 2 CUPS

7 bacon slices
2 garlic cloves, minced
8 ounces cream cheese, softened
1/4 cup half-and-half
4 ounces bleu cheese, crumbled
2 tablespoons chopped chives

- COOK THE BACON in a skillet over medium-high heat for about 7 minutes or until nearly crisp; drain. Add the garlic to the skillet and cook for 3 minutes or until the bacon is crisp. Remove from the heat. Crumble the bacon.

- Beat the cream cheese in a mixing bowl until fluffy. Add the half-and-half and beat until well combined. Stir in the bacon mixture, bleu cheese and chives. Spoon the mixture into a 2-cup baking dish. Cover with foil.

- Bake at 350 degrees for 30 minutes or until heated through. Serve with thick-cut potato chips and crackers.

- NOTE: You may prepare the dip 1 day in advance and refrigerate; bring to room temperature before baking.

Thai Crab Dip

MAKES 20 SERVINGS

1 serrano chile, seeded and
   chopped
1 garlic clove, minced
1 tablespoon thinly sliced
   fresh lemon grass from
   the lowest 3 inches of
   the stalk
2 teaspoons grated
   lemon zest
2 teaspoons Asian fish
   sauce
2 tablespoons fresh
   lime juice
Salt to taste
2 cups lump crab meat,
   picked over
3 tablespoons slivered basil
   leaves
2 tablespoons torn fresh
   cilantro
1/4 cup canned unsweetened
   coconut milk
3 medium heads Belgian
   endive

- COMBINE THE CHILE, garlic, lemon grass, lemon zest, fish sauce, lime juice and salt in a large bowl and mix well. Add the crab meat, basil and cilantro.

- Stir the coconut milk well to combine and pour over the crab mixture. Toss gently to combine.

- Serve with leaves of Belgian endive and crackers.

- NOTE: You may purchase lemon grass at most Asian markets, especially those specializing in Thai products. Lemon grass is also referred to as citronella and sereh.

Hot Sausage Dip

MAKES 9 CUPS

*2 pounds hot bulk pork
  sausage*
*32 ounces cream cheese,
  softened*
*1 (4-ounce) can chopped
  green chiles*
*6 ounces pickled jalapeño
  slices, drained, chopped*

- COOK THE SAUSAGE in a large skillet over medium-high heat, stirring until browned and crumbly; drain. Add the cream cheese to the skillet. Reduce the heat to low and cook until the cheese is melted. Add the green chiles and jalapeños and mix well. Spoon into a rectangular baking dish.

- Bake at 350 degrees for 30 minutes. Serve with tortilla chips or corn chips.

Baked Spinach Dip

MAKES 4 ½ CUPS

*1 (10-ounce) package
  frozen chopped spinach,
  thawed, drained*
*8 ounces cream cheese,
  softened*
*8 ounces shredded Monterey
  Jack cheese*
⅓ cup half-and-half
*2 medium tomatoes,
  chopped*
⅓ cup minced onion
*1 tablespoon minced
  jalapeño peppers*
Dash of Tabasco sauce

- COMBINE THE SPINACH, cream cheese, Monterey Jack cheese, half-and-half, tomatoes, onion, jalapeños and Tabasco sauce in a large bowl and mix well. Spoon into a greased baking dish.

- Bake at 400 degrees for 20 to 25 minutes or until bubbly. Serve with tortilla chips.

Shrimp Dip

1 (4-ounce) can deveined
  shrimp
¹/₂ cup finely chopped onion
¹/₂ cup finely chopped celery
1 cup sour cream
8 ounces cream cheese,
  softened
Juice of 1 lemon
Dash of Worcestershire
  sauce

- MASH THE SHRIMP in a medium bowl with a fork. Add the onion, celery, sour cream, cream cheese, lemon juice and Worcestershire sauce and mix well.

- Chill, covered, in the refrigerator. Serve with crackers.

Lake Burton Dip

1 cup sour cream
1 envelope Italian salad
  dressing mix
1 tablespoon mayonnaise
2 tablespoons lemon juice
¹/₂ avocado, chopped
¹/₂ tomato, chopped
Dash of hot pepper sauce

- COMBINE THE SOUR cream, salad dressing mix, mayonnaise, lemon juice, avocado, tomato and hot pepper sauce in a small serving bowl and mix well.

- Chill, covered, until ready to serve. Serve with potato chips or bite-size fresh vegetables.

Curry Dip for Vegetables

1 cup mayonnaise
1 teaspoon horseradish
1 teaspoon grated onion
1 teaspoon white wine
    vinegar
1 teaspoon (scant) curry
    powder

- COMBINE THE MAYONNAISE, horseradish, onion, vinegar and curry powder in a bowl and mix well. Refrigerate, covered, for 24 hours or up to a week. Serve with bite-size vegetables.

- NOTE: You may use dried onion flakes instead of fresh onion. Mix 1/4 teaspoon onion flakes with 1 1/2 teaspoons white wine vinegar before combining with remaining ingredients.

Mexican Hat Dance

MAKES 12 SERVINGS

2 cups sour cream
1 envelope taco
    seasoning mix
2 (9-ounce) cans bean dip
3 (10-ounce) containers
    refrigerated guacamole
2 cups shredded Cheddar
    cheese
2 large tomatoes, finely
    chopped, drained
1 (4-ounce) can chopped
    green chiles, drained
1 (4-ounce) can chopped
    black olives, drained

- COMBINE THE SOUR cream and taco seasoning mix in a small bowl and mix well. Layer the bean dip, guacamole, seasoned sour cream, Cheddar cheese, tomatoes, green chiles and black olives in the order listed in a large rectangular glass dish.

- Refrigerate, covered, until serving time. Serve with tortilla chips or corn chips.

Spicy Black Bean Salsa

MAKES 80 SERVINGS

2 (15-ounce) cans black
    beans, drained, rinsed
1 (16-ounce) can corn,
    drained
$1/2$ cup chopped fresh
    cilantro
6 tablespoons lime juice
6 tablespoons vegetable oil
$1/2$ cup minced red onion
$1^1/2$ teaspoons ground cumin
1 (16-ounce) can chopped
    tomatoes
$1/2$ (10-ounce) can chopped
    tomatoes with green chiles
$1/2$ cup medium-hot picante
    sauce
Salt and pepper to taste

- COMBINE THE BLACK beans, corn, cilantro, lime juice, oil, red onion, cumin, tomatoes, tomatoes with green chiles, picante sauce, salt and pepper in a large serving bowl and mix well.

- Refrigerate, covered, for 24 hours, stirring occasionally. Serve with tortilla chips, or as an accompaniment to a Mexican or southwestern entrée.

Poor Man's Butter

MAKES 12 SERVINGS

4 tomatoes, chopped
4 avocados, chopped
2 bunches green onions,
  thinly sliced
1 1/2 teaspoons salt
2 tablespoons minced
  fresh cilantro
2 tablespoons vegetable oil
1/3 cup red wine vinegar

- PLACE THE TOMATOES in a strainer or colander and let stand for 15 minutes or longer to drain.

- Combine the tomatoes with the avocados, green onions, salt, cilantro, oil and vinegar in a medium bowl and mix well. Chill, covered, for 1 hour. Serve as a dip with tortilla chips.

Caviar Pie

MAKES 3 1/2 CUPS

8 ounces cream cheese,
  softened
2 1/2 teaspoons grated onion
1/4 cup mayonnaise
1 1/2 teaspoons
  Worcestershire sauce
1 1/2 teaspoons lemon juice
2 (2-ounce) jars black
  caviar, rinsed and drained
2 or 3 hard-cooked eggs,
  grated
1 cup parsley, chopped
6 green onions, thinly sliced
1 (2-ounce) jar red caviar,
  rinsed and drained

- COMBINE THE CREAM cheese, onion, mayonnaise, Worcestershire sauce and lemon juice in a bowl and mix well. Spread over a pie dish in a 1-inch layer. Spread the black caviar over the cream cheese mixture. Sprinkle the grated egg over the black caviar.

- Combine the parsley and green onions in a small bowl and mix well. Spread the green onion mixture over the grated egg, leaving a central circle showing. Put a spoonful of the red caviar in the center. Chill, covered, for at least 1 hour before serving. Serve with melba toast rounds.

Shrimp Mold

1 (10-ounce) can she-crab
   soup or lobster Newburg
   soup
6 ounces cream cheese
1 envelope unflavored
   gelatin
$1/4$ cup cold water
1 tablespoon lemon juice
1 cup mayonnaise
1 cup chopped celery
2 dozen medium shrimp,
   peeled, cooked, chopped
4 green onions, thinly sliced
$1/4$ teaspoon curry powder
Whole cooked peeled
   shrimp
Parsley sprigs

- MICROWAVE THE SOUP and cream cheese in a microwave-safe bowl or heat in a double boiler over simmering water until cheese is melted, stirring until mixture is blended and creamy.

- Sprinkle the gelatin over the cold water in a bowl. Let stand until softened. Stir into the soup mixture. Add the lemon juice, mayonnaise, celery, chopped shrimp, green onions and curry powder and mix well.

- Spoon into a greased fish-shaped mold. Chill, covered, for 4 to 5 hours or until firm. Unmold onto a serving platter and garnish with whole cooked shrimp and parsley sprigs. Serve with crackers.

Goat Cheese and Sun-Dried Tomato Torta

MAKES ABOUT 5 CUPS

1 cup (2 sticks) unsalted butter, softened
12 ounces Montrachet goat cheese
8 ounces cream cheese, softened
1 cup Basil Pesto (below)
1 (7-ounce) jar oil-pack sun-dried tomatoes, drained, chopped

- BEAT THE BUTTER, goat cheese and cream cheese in a large mixing bowl at medium speed until well mixed and fluffy, scraping the side of the bowl often. Line a 1-quart bowl or mold with plastic wrap. Spoon a third of the cheese mixture into the bottom of the bowl and spread evenly. Cover with half of the Basil Pesto. Repeat the layers, ending with a layer of the cheese mixture.

- Refrigerate, covered, for at least 1 hour to firm up, or until serving time. Invert the bowl onto a platter and remove the plastic wrap. Cover the top with the sun-dried tomatoes. Serve with crackers.

Basil Pesto

MAKES ABOUT 1 CUP

2 cups lightly packed fresh basil leaves
1/2 cup lightly packed fresh parsley
1/2 cup olive oil
3 tablespoons pine nuts
2 garlic cloves, crushed
2 tablespoons unsalted butter, softened
1/4 cup freshly grated Parmesan cheese
Salt to taste

- COMBINE THE BASIL, parsley, olive oil, pine nuts and garlic in a blender or food processor. Process until the mixture is a fine paste.

- Stir in the butter and Parmesan cheese with a spoon. Season with salt to taste. You may store pesto, covered, in the freezer.

Vidalia Onion Spread

MAKES **4 1/2 CUPS**

2 cups coarsely chopped
    Vidalia onions
1 cup mayonnaise
1 1/2 cups shredded Cheddar
    cheese
Paprika to taste

- COMBINE THE ONIONS, mayonnaise and cheese in a bowl and mix well. Spoon into a 1-quart baking dish. Sprinkle with paprika. Bake at 350 degrees for 30 to 40 minutes. Blot the top with a paper towel to remove excess oil. Serve hot with shredded wheat crackers.

- NOTE: You may also use this cooled spread as a filling for hollowed-out cherry tomatoes. Broil for 5 minutes before serving.

Dinner Party Bleu Cheese Spread

MAKES **1 1/2 CUPS**

8 ounces cream cheese
4 ounces bleu cheese
1/2 teaspoon garlic powder
Dash of Worcestershire
    sauce
Salt and white pepper to
    taste
Chives to taste

- COMBINE THE CREAM cheese, bleu cheese, garlic powder, Worcestershire sauce, salt, pepper and chives in a food processor. Process until thoroughly mixed. Spoon into a serving dish. Chill, covered, for 1 day to allow flavors to develop. Serve with celery or crackers.

- NOTE: You may use nonfat cream cheese in this recipe.

Vegetable Spread

1 envelope unflavored
  gelatin
¹/₄ cup cold water
¹/₄ cup boiling water
3 ounces reduced-fat cream
  cheese
2 cups reduced-fat
  mayonnaise
1 tablespoon vinegar
Dash of salt and pepper
1 small onion, finely
  chopped
2 tomatoes, finely chopped,
  drained
1 green bell pepper,
  finely chopped
1 cucumber, peeled,
  finely chopped
1 cup finely chopped celery

- SPRINKLE THE GELATIN over the cold water in a medium bowl. Add the boiling water and stir to completely dissolve gelatin.

- Add the cream cheese to the hot gelatin mixture and mix well. Cool the mixture.

- Add the mayonnaise, vinegar, salt, pepper, onion, tomatoes, bell pepper, cucumber and celery and mix well. Spoon into a gelatin mold. Chill, covered, until firm. Serve with chicken-flavor crackers.

Salmon Mousse

MAKES ABOUT 8 CUPS

1 cup minced onions
3 tablespoons butter
1 1/2 cups clam juice,
    whitefish stock, or
    court bouillon
1 1/2 envelopes unflavored
    gelatin
1/3 cup dry white wine
3 cups flaked cooked
    salmon
Salt, pepper and lemon juice
    to taste
1/3 cup mayonnaise
1/3 cup heavy cream
Cucumber Sauce (page 43)

- SAUTÉ THE ONIONS in butter in a medium skillet until soft. Add the strained clam juice and simmer for 5 minutes.

- Sprinkle the gelatin over the wine and let stand for 5 minutes. Add to the skillet and stir until the gelatin dissolves.

- Combine a third of the salmon and a third of the gelatin mixture in a blender. Process until finely chopped and thoroughly mixed. Repeat with the remaining salmon and gelatin mixture. Transfer to a bowl. Season with salt, pepper and lemon juice.

- Mix the mayonnaise and cream in a small bowl. Add to the salmon mixture and mix well. Spoon the mousse into a greased fish-shaped mold or other gelatin mold.

- Refrigerate, covered, until set. Unmold onto a serving platter. Serve with Cucumber Sauce. Surround with crackers.

Cucumber Sauce

5 large cucumbers
1½ teaspoons salt
1 cup mayonnaise
1 cup sour cream
1 tablespoon Dijon mustard
2 tablespoons chopped
    fresh dill
Salt and pepper to taste

- PEEL THE CUCUMBERS and cut into halves lengthwise. Scoop out the seeds with a spoon and discard.

- Slice the cucumbers thinly, place in a bowl and sprinkle with the salt. Chill, covered, for 1 hour. Drain in a colander, pressing out excess moisture. Wrap the cucumbers in a clean dish towel and squeeze dry.

- Combine the mayonnaise, sour cream, Dijon mustard and dill in a bowl. Add the cucumbers and mix well. Season with salt and pepper. Spoon into a small serving bowl. Serve with Salmon Mousse (page 42) or other favorite salmon dish.

Soups and Salads

Artichoke Soup

1 (14-ounce) can artichoke
  hearts
2 tablespoons butter
1 onion, chopped
2 tablespoons flour
2 cups chicken broth
2 tablespoons chopped
  parsley
1¼ cups half-and-half
Salt, garlic powder and
  seasoned pepper to taste
Chopped chives

- DRAIN THE ARTICHOKES, reserving the liquid. Chop the artichokes. Heat the butter in a medium skillet. Sauté the onion in the skillet. Add the flour and mix well. Cook for 2 minutes, stirring constantly.

- Add the reserved artichoke liquid, chicken broth, artichokes and parsley and mix well. Cook for 5 minutes, stirring frequently.

- Purée the mixture in a blender. Return the puréed mixture to the skillet. Add the half-and-half, salt, garlic powder and seasoned pepper. Cook until heated through. Serve hot or cold, garnished with chopped chives.

- NOTE: You may easily double this recipe, and store, covered, in the freezer.

Broccoli Swiss Soup

MAKES 12 SERVINGS

2$^1/_2$ pounds broccoli
$^1/_4$ cup ($^1/_2$ stick) butter
1 cup chopped leeks
$^1/_4$ cup flour
4 cups chicken broth
1 cup half-and-half
1$^1/_2$ cups shredded
   Swiss cheese
$^1/_8$ teaspoon nutmeg
Salt and pepper to taste

- CUT 2 CUPS of florets from the broccoli. Cut the remaining broccoli into 1-inch pieces. Cook the florets and chopped broccoli separately in boiling water until tender. Rinse in cold water to stop cooking process; drain. Set aside.

- Melt the butter in a large saucepan. Sauté the leeks in the melted butter for 3 minutes or until tender. Stir in the flour and cook for 1 minute, stirring constantly. Remove the pan from the heat and stir in the chicken broth. Reduce the heat to low and simmer for 5 minutes, stirring occasionally. Add the chopped broccoli.

- Purée the soup in a blender in batches until smooth. Return the puréed mixture to the saucepan and add the half-and-half and Swiss cheese.

- Cook over low heat until the cheese is melted, stirring occasionally. Season with the nutmeg, salt and pepper. Add the broccoli florets and mix well. Cook until heated through. Serve immediately.

Creamy Carrot and Potato Soup

2 tablespoons butter
2 leeks, white part only,
  sliced
4 cups cubed peeled
  potatoes
3 cups sliced peeled carrots
6 cups chicken broth
2 teaspoons salt
1/8 teaspoon white pepper
2 cups half-and-half
Shredded carrot

- MELT THE BUTTER in a large saucepan over medium heat. Add the leeks and cook for several minutes, stirring occasionally. Add the potatoes, sliced carrots, chicken broth, salt and pepper; bring to a boil. Reduce the heat to low and simmer for 30 minutes or until the vegetables are tender.

- Purée the soup in batches in a blender. Return the puréed mixture to the saucepan and add the half-and-half. Cook over low heat until heated through. Garnish with shredded carrot.

Italian Minestrone

2½ pounds blade chuck
  roast or meaty soup
  bones
2½ quarts water
2 teaspoons salt
1 small onion, sliced
½ cup celery leaves
1 bay leaf
2 slices bacon, diced
1½ cups cooked dried or
  canned kidney beans
½ cup chopped fresh
  green beans
½ cup diced celery
½ cup fresh or frozen
  green peas
½ cup thinly sliced zucchini
½ cup thinly sliced carrots
¼ cup diced onion
¼ cup chopped parsley
1 garlic clove, minced
½ cup (2 ounces) uncooked
  elbow macaroni
1 (6-ounce) can tomato
  paste
1 cup cola
1 tablespoon olive oil
1 tablespoon Worcestershire
  sauce
1 teaspoon Italian seasoning
1 teaspoon salt
¼ teaspoon pepper
Grated Parmesan cheese

- COMBINE THE ROAST, water, 2 teaspoons salt, sliced onion, celery leaves and bay leaf in a large pan. Simmer, covered, over medium heat for 2½ hours or until meat is tender.

- Strain the broth, which should measure about 2 quarts. Set aside the meat and bones and discard other solids. Add ice cubes to the broth. Skim the broth. Chop the meat, discarding the fat and bones. Meat should measure about 2 cups.

- Combine the broth and meat in a 5- to 6-quart stockpot and place over low heat.

- Fry the bacon in a skillet over medium-high heat until crisp. Add the bacon with the drippings, kidney beans, green beans, ½ cup celery, peas, zucchini, carrots, ¼ cup onion, parsley, garlic, macaroni, tomato paste, cola, olive oil, Worcestershire sauce, Italian seasoning, 1 teaspoon salt and pepper to the broth and meat in the stockpot.

- Simmer, covered, for 30 minutes or until the vegetables and macaroni are tender. Serve sprinkled with Parmesan cheese if desired.

Crab and Oyster Gumbo

MAKES **10** TO **12** SERVINGS

¹/₄ cup vegetable oil
¹/₂ pound chorizo, cut into
    ¹/₄-inch slices
¹/₂ pound smoked ham,
    cut into ¹/₂-inch cubes
1 large onion, chopped
3 garlic cloves, minced
1 large green bell pepper,
    chopped
1 large red bell pepper,
    chopped
2 celery ribs, chopped
1 (14-ounce) can plum
    tomatoes
6 cups fish stock or
    chicken broth
3 bay leaves
1 teaspoon hot paprika
¹/₂ teaspoon thyme
¹/₂ teaspoon oregano
¹/₄ teaspoon cayenne
    pepper
1 teaspoon salt
¹/₄ teaspoon pepper
4 ounces okra, cut into
    ¹/₂-inch slices
¹/₂ cup sliced green onions
4 dozen oysters, drained,
    liquid strained and
    reserved
2 tablespoons filé powder
    (optional)
1 pound lump crab meat
Hot steamed white rice

- HEAT THE OIL in a heavy Dutch oven or ovenproof casserole over medium-high heat. Add the chorizo and ham and cook for 8 minutes or until browned. Remove the meat with a slotted spoon and set aside.

- Add the onion and garlic to the pan. Cook for 5 minutes or until tender, stirring frequently. Add the bell peppers and celery to the pan and cook for 5 minutes or until the vegetables begin to soften.

- Add the chorizo, ham, undrained tomatoes, fish stock, bay leaves, paprika, thyme, oregano, cayenne pepper, salt and pepper. Break up the tomatoes with a spoon. Simmer for 45 minutes, stirring occasionally.

- You may hold the gumbo for a while at this point until ready to add the remaining ingredients, or you may refrigerate, covered, for up to 1 day.

- Add the okra and green onions and mix well. Simmer for 10 minutes. Stir in the reserved oyster liquid, filé powder, oysters and crab meat. Simmer for about 5 minutes or until the oysters begin to curl. Serve immediately over hot white rice.

Red Chili

2 pounds coarsely ground beef
3 tablespoons olive oil
1 large onion, chopped
1 large red bell pepper, chopped
1 large green bell pepper, chopped
4 garlic cloves, minced
2 (28-ounce) cans plum tomatoes
1 (24-ounce) can vegetable juice cocktail
2 tablespoons chili powder
1 tablespoon basil
1 tablespoon oregano
$1/2$ teaspoon sugar
$1/4$ teaspoon ground cumin
Salt and pepper to taste
2 (15-ounce) cans red kidney beans

- COOK THE GROUND beef in a very small amount of the olive oil in a skillet over high heat, stirring until brown and crumbly; drain.

- Sauté the onion, bell peppers and garlic in the remaining olive oil in a stockpot until tender. Add the ground beef, undrained tomatoes, vegetable juice, chili powder, basil, oregano, sugar, cumin, salt and pepper to the stockpot and mix well.

- Cook, covered, over low heat for 3 hours. Adjust seasonings. Add the kidney beans and cook until heated through.

Italian Fresh Vegetable Soup

MAKES ABOUT 3 QUARTS

1/2 cup olive oil

3 tablespoons butter

1 cup thinly sliced yellow
   onion

1 cup chopped carrots

1 cup chopped celery

2 cups (about 2 medium)
   chopped peeled potatoes

2 cups chopped zucchini

1 cup (about 8 ounces)
   chopped green beans

3 cups shredded cabbage

6 cups homemade beef
   stock, or 2 cups canned
   broth plus 4 cups water

2/3 cup canned plum
   tomatoes with juice,
   chopped

Salt to taste

1 1/2 cups cooked dried or
   canned cannellini beans

1/3 cup freshly grated
   Parmesan cheese

- HEAT THE OLIVE oil and butter in a large saucepan over medium heat. Cook the onion in the saucepan until tender, stirring occasionally. Add the carrots and cook for 2 to 3 minutes, stirring occasionally. Add the celery and cook for 2 to 3 minutes, stirring occasionally. Add the potatoes, zucchini and green beans, adding more butter if needed and stirring occasionally. Add the cabbage and cook for 6 minutes, stirring occasionally.

- Add the beef stock, tomatoes and salt. Cook, covered, over low heat for 3 hours or longer. Add the beans during the last 15 minutes of cooking. Add the cheese just before serving.

- NOTE: For a homemade beef stock, see Italian Minestrone, page 49.

Swan Coach House Cream of Wild Rice Soup

MAKES ABOUT 16 CUPS

2 large onions, finely
   chopped
2 carrots, finely chopped
2 celery ribs, finely chopped
2 cups finely chopped ham
1 cup (2 sticks) butter
1/2 cup flour
16 cups (1 gallon) chicken
   broth
Salt and white pepper
   to taste
2 cups light cream or
   half-and-half
4 cups cooked wild rice

- SAUTÉ THE ONIONS, carrots, celery and ham in the butter in a 4- to 5-quart saucepan over medium heat for 3 minutes or until tender-crisp.

- Sift in the flour, a small amount at a time, stirring until well mixed. Add the chicken broth slowly, stirring until well blended. Season with salt and white pepper.

- Cook until the mixture thickens, stirring constantly. Add the half-and-half and wild rice. Cook until heated through. Serve immediately.

Cold Tomato Soup

1/2 cup (1 stick) butter
2 tablespoons olive oil
1 large onion, thinly sliced
1/2 teaspoon dried thyme
1/2 teaspoon dried basil
Salt and pepper to taste
2 1/2 pounds ripe tomatoes,
    cored, or 28 ounces
    canned plum tomatoes
3 tablespoons tomato paste
1/4 cup flour
3 3/4 cups chicken broth
1 teaspoon sugar
1 cup heavy cream
1/4 cup (1/2 stick) butter
Sour cream
Cucumber slices

- HEAT THE 1/2 CUP butter and olive oil in a large saucepan over medium-high heat. Add the onion and stir to coat. Add the thyme, basil, salt and pepper. Sauté until the onion is tender. Coarsely chop the tomatoes. Add the tomatoes and tomato paste to the onion mixture and mix well. Simmer for 10 minutes.

- Combine the flour with about 1/3 cup of the chicken broth in a small bowl and stir until mixture is smooth. Stir into the tomato mixture. Cook until slightly thickened, stirring frequently. Add the remaining chicken broth and simmer for 30 minutes, stirring frequently, as the mixture will stick.

- Purée the mixture in a blender in batches. Return the puréed mixture to the pan. Add the sugar and cream and simmer for 5 minutes. Add the 1/4 cup butter and cook until the butter melts. Let cool. Chill, covered, until ready to serve. Garnish with sour cream and cucumber slices.

- NOTE: You may also serve this soup hot.

Cold and Spicy Moroccan Tomato Soup

MAKES 4 SERVINGS

5 garlic cloves, minced
2¹/₂ teaspoons paprika
Cayenne pepper to taste
1¹/₂ teaspoons ground
   cumin
4 teaspoons olive oil
2¹/₄ pounds tomatoes,
   seeded and chopped
¹/₄ cup cilantro, chopped
1 tablespoon white wine
   vinegar
2 tablespoons plus
   2 teaspoons fresh
   lemon juice
3 tablespoons water
2 celery ribs, diced
Salt to taste
Cilantro leaves

- COMBINE THE GARLIC, paprika, cayenne pepper, cumin and olive oil in a small saucepan and mix well. Cook over low heat for 2 minutes, stirring constantly. Remove from the heat.

- Process the tomatoes in a blender or food processor to a chunky texture, pulsing on and off.

- Combine the tomatoes with the garlic mixture, ¹/₄ cup cilantro, white wine vinegar, lemon juice, water, celery and salt in a large bowl and mix well.

- Refrigerate, covered, until very cold. Garnish with cilantro leaves.

Blender Borscht

2 (15-ounce) cans cut beets
1/2 cup chopped onion
3 tablespoons lemon juice
1 teaspoon salt
2 tablespoons tomato paste
2 (10-ounce) cans beef
    consommé
Sour cream
Chopped mint or parsley

- COMBINE THE UNDRAINED beets and onion in a blender and process at high speed until mixture is puréed.

- Pour the beet-onion mixture into a saucepan. Add the lemon juice, salt, tomato paste and beef consommé and mix well.

- Bring to a boil over medium to medium-high heat. Reduce heat to low and simmer for 4 to 5 minutes. Remove from heat. Let cool. Refrigerate, covered, until completely chilled. Serve cold, topped with sour cream and chopped mint or parsley.

Gingered Carrot Vichyssoise

2 tablespoons butter
5 carrots, peeled and
    coarsely chopped
1 small onion, coarsely
    chopped
8 cups chicken stock
1 potato, peeled and
    quartered
$1/2$-inch piece of fresh
    ginger, peeled and sliced
1 tablespoon salt
1 teaspoon white pepper
$3/4$ cup heavy cream
Chopped chives

• HEAT THE BUTTER in a stockpot and add the carrots and onion. Cook over low heat for 10 minutes, stirring occasionally.

• Add the chicken stock, potato, ginger, salt and white pepper. Simmer, uncovered, for 45 minutes. Strain the mixture, returning the liquid to the stockpot and reserving the solids.

• Purée reserved solids in a blender or food processor. Return the puréed mixture to the stockpot and mix well. Bring to a boil over medium-high heat. Reduce heat to low.

• Add the cream and simmer for 5 minutes. Remove from the heat. Let cool. Refrigerate, covered, until chilled. Serve garnished with chopped chives.

Cucumber Vichyssoise

2 cups chopped unpeeled
  cucumber
$1/4$ cup chopped onion
$1/2$ cup chopped peeled
  potato
2 cups chicken stock
1 teaspoon chopped fresh
  parsley
$1/8$ teaspoon pepper
$1/4$ teaspoon dry mustard
Salt and pepper to taste
1 cup heavy cream
Chopped parsley

- COMBINE THE CUCUMBER, onion, potato, chicken stock, 1 teaspoon fresh parsley, $1/8$ teaspoon pepper and dry mustard in a saucepan. Cook, covered, over medium-high heat for 10 minutes or until the potato is tender. Drain and reserve 1 cup of the liquid.

- Purée the remaining liquid with the vegetables in a blender or food processor. Combine with the reserved liquid in a large bowl and mix well. Season with salt and pepper. Refrigerate, covered, until completely chilled. Stir in the cream before serving. Serve garnished with parsley.

Gazpacho

1 (32-ounce) can vegetable
  juice cocktail
1 tablespoon olive oil
2 tablespoons red wine
  vinegar
1 chicken bouillon cube
1 garlic clove
$1/8$ teaspoon pepper
$1/2$ teaspoon salt
3 dashes of hot pepper
  sauce
1 small ripe tomato,
  chopped
1 cup chopped peeled
  cucumber
$1/4$ cup chopped green bell
  pepper
$1/4$ medium onion, sliced
Sour cream (optional)

• COMBINE 1 CUP of the vegetable juice,
  olive oil, red wine vinegar, bouillon cube,
  garlic, pepper, salt and hot pepper sauce
  in a blender or food processor container.
  Process for a few seconds.

• Add the tomato, cucumber, bell pepper and
  onion and process just until chopped. Add
  the remaining vegetable juice and mix well.
  Pour into a large bowl.

• Refrigerate, covered, until ready to serve.
  You may serve with a dollop of sour cream.

Chilled Red Pepper Soup

MAKES 6 SERVINGS

4 leeks, white part only,
   chopped
4 red bell peppers, seeded
   and chopped
3 tablespoons butter
1 cup defatted chicken stock
1/4 teaspoon thyme
1/2 teaspoon crumbled
   bay leaf
3 cups defatted chicken
   stock
1 cup sour cream
Salt and freshly ground
   white pepper to taste
Red bell pepper strips

- COOK THE LEEKS and 4 bell peppers in the butter in a large saucepan, covered, over low heat for 15 minutes, stirring occasionally. Add the 1 cup chicken stock, thyme and bay leaf and bring to a boil. Reduce heat and simmer, covered, for 30 minutes.

- Purée the mixture in a blender or food processor. Pour puréed mixture into a large bowl and add the 3 cups chicken stock and sour cream. Season with salt and white pepper. Refrigerate, covered, until chilled. Serve garnished with julienne strips of bell pepper.

Swan Coach House Strawberry Soup

MAKES 24 SERVINGS

2 quarts fresh strawberries
4 cups sour cream
2 cups milk
1 cup sugar
4 teaspoons vanilla extract
1/4 cup lemon juice
1 1/2 (1-liter) bottles
   ginger ale

- PURÉE THE STRAWBERRIES, sour cream, milk, sugar, vanilla and lemon juice in a blender. Chill, covered, until ready to serve. Before serving, add the ginger ale and mix well.

Green Bean and
Red Onion Salad with Chèvre

1 pound fresh green beans
1/2 cup light olive oil
3 tablespoons raspberry
   vinegar
1 tablespoon chopped
   fresh dill
1 teaspoon salt
1/4 teaspoon pepper
1 1/2 tablespoons sugar
1 red onion, sliced into
   thin rings
3 Granny Smith apples,
   cored and thinly sliced
4 ounces chèvre, cut into
   thin wedges
Toasted walnuts (optional)

- COOK THE GREEN beans with enough water to cover in a saucepan for 3 to 4 minutes or until tender-crisp; drain. Plunge the green beans into cold water to stop the cooking process.

- Combine the olive oil, raspberry vinegar, dill, salt, pepper and sugar in a large bowl and mix well. Add the green beans and onion; stir to coat. Refrigerate, covered, for at least 8 hours. Add the apples and chèvre and toss to coat.

- NOTE: You may drain the dressing from the green beans and onion, arrange them on serving plates and top with the apples and chèvre. Drizzle with the dressing. You may also sprinkle the salad with toasted walnuts.

The Lark and the Dove's Caesar Salad

MAKES **2** SERVINGS

1 medium garlic clove
1 anchovy fillet
Dash of Tabasco sauce
    (optional)
1 tablespoon Parmesan
    cheese
1 teaspoon Worcestershire
    sauce
1/4 teaspoon dry mustard
1 egg yolk
Juice of 1/2 lemon
3 tablespoons olive oil
1 tablespoon red wine
    vinegar
2 handfuls washed, dried,
    torn romaine lettuce
2 tablespoons Parmesan
    cheese
1/2 cup seasoned croutons
Freshly ground pepper

- MINCE THE GARLIC and anchovy. Combine the garlic and anchovy with the Tabasco sauce, 1 tablespoon Parmesan cheese, Worcestershire sauce, dry mustard, egg yolk and lemon juice in a large bowl and mix well.

- Add a mixture of the olive oil and red wine vinegar and mix well. Add the lettuce and toss to coat. Add the 2 tablespoons Parmesan cheese and croutons and toss well.

- Serve on chilled plates. Top with additional Parmesan cheese, if desired, and freshly ground pepper.

No-Stir Coleslaw

1 large head cabbage
1 large sweet onion,
   thinly sliced
1 large green bell pepper,
   thinly sliced
2 carrots, shredded
   (optional)
$^1/_2$ to 1 cup sugar
$^3/_4$ cup vegetable oil
1 cup vinegar
1 teaspoon dry mustard
1 teaspoon celery seeds
Salt to taste

- SHRED THE CABBAGE and place in a large bowl. Layer the onion, bell pepper and carrots over the top of the cabbage. Sprinkle with the sugar; do not stir.

- Combine the oil, vinegar, dry mustard, celery seeds and salt in a saucepan and mix well. Bring to a boil over medium heat. Pour immediately over the vegetables; do not stir. Refrigerate, covered, for at least 4 hours before serving.

- NOTE: You may store the coleslaw, covered, in the refrigerator for several days.

Lemon Slaw

Lemon Dressing
$1/2$ cup mayonnaise
$1/2$ cup sour cream
$1/4$ cup fresh lemon juice
2 tablespoons Dijon mustard
2 tablespoons olive oil
2 tablespoons sugar
1 tablespoon white wine
   vinegar
1 tablespoon horseradish
1 teaspoon salt
$1/2$ teaspoon celery seeds
$1/2$ teaspoon pepper

Coleslaw
8 cups (about $1 1/2$ pounds)
   shredded cabbage
$1/2$ red bell pepper,
   cut into julienne strips
$1/2$ green bell pepper,
   cut into julienne strips
$1/4$ red onion, cut into
   julienne strips
1 carrot, shredded
2 tablespoons chopped
   parsley
2 teaspoons grated
   lemon zest

- FOR THE DRESSING, combine the mayonnaise, sour cream, lemon juice, Dijon mustard, olive oil, sugar, white wine vinegar, horseradish, salt, celery seeds and pepper in a bowl or a jar with a tight-fitting lid and mix well. Refrigerate, covered, until chilled.

- For the coleslaw, combine the cabbage, bell peppers, onion, carrot, parsley and lemon zest in a large bowl and mix well. Add the dressing and toss to coat.

Chinese Slaw

2 (3-ounce) packages ramen
  noodles
1 large head cabbage,
  shredded, or 2 (10-ounce)
  packages shredded
  cabbage
8 green onions, thinly sliced
3/4 cup sliced almonds,
  toasted
1/2 cup sesame seeds,
  toasted
1 cup vegetable oil
1 garlic clove, minced
1 tablespoon peanut butter
1/3 cup sugar
1/8 teaspoon Chinese
  mustard
1/4 cup soy sauce
1/2 cup rice wine vinegar
1/8 teaspoon dry mustard
1/8 teaspoon pepper

• CRUSH THE RAMEN noodles and discard
the seasoning packets. Combine the ramen
noodles with the cabbage, green onions,
almonds and sesame seeds in a large bowl
and mix well.

• Combine the oil, garlic, peanut butter, sugar,
Chinese mustard, soy sauce, rice wine
vinegar, dry mustard and pepper in
a bowl or a jar with a tight-fitting lid and
mix well. Pour over cabbage mixture and
toss to coat. Serve immediately.

Snow Pea Salad

8 ounces fresh snow peas,
  strings removed
Salt to taste
2 tablespoons sesame seeds
8 ounces mushrooms,
  stemmed, sliced
1 large red bell pepper,
  seeded and cut into strips
1 garlic clove, minced
1/3 cup vegetable oil
2 tablespoons white wine
  vinegar
1 tablespoon lemon juice
1 tablespoon sugar
1/2 teaspoon salt

- BLANCH THE SNOW peas in 2 quarts of boiling salted water for 1 minute; drain. Plunge snow peas into cold water. Drain well and pat dry with paper towels. Cut the snow peas into halves on the diagonal and place in a medium salad bowl.

- Toast the sesame seeds in a small skillet over medium heat for about 1 minute, shaking the skillet constantly. Set aside.

- Add the mushrooms and bell pepper to the snow peas. Combine the garlic, oil, white wine vinegar, lemon juice, sugar and 1/2 teaspoon salt in a bowl or a jar with a tight-fitting lid and mix well. Pour over the vegetables. Sprinkle with the sesame seeds. Toss to mix.

Hot Spinach Salad

1 pound fresh spinach
8 slices bacon
3 tablespoons brown sugar
$1/3$ cup sliced green onions
Salt to taste
3 tablespoons white vinegar
$1/4$ teaspoon dry mustard

- RINSE the spinach and pat dry. Refrigerate until chilled. Tear the spinach into small pieces and place in a salad bowl.

- Just before serving, chop the bacon and cook it in a skillet over medium-high heat until crisp. Reduce the heat to low.

- Add the brown sugar, green onions, salt, vinegar and dry mustard to the skillet. Bring to a boil. Remove from the heat and pour over the spinach. Toss to coat.

- NOTE: You may make the dressing in advance and reheat it when ready to toss over the spinach.

Cornucopia Salad

Sugared Almonds
1/2 cup sliced almonds
3 tablespoons sugar

Salad
1 medium head green leaf
  lettuce
4 green onions, sliced
1 (8-ounce) can mandarin
  oranges, drained
1 avocado, sliced
1 Granny Smith apple,
  sliced
1/4 cup dried cranberries
1/2 cup crumbled bleu
  cheese

Oil and Vinegar Dressing
1/4 cup vegetable oil
1 tablespoon fresh parsley
2 tablespoons sugar
2 tablespoons white wine or
  apple cider vinegar
1/2 teaspoon salt
1/2 teaspoon pepper

- FOR THE ALMONDS, place the almonds in a small skillet. Sprinkle with the sugar. Heat over medium heat until the sugar melts and the almonds brown. Pour the hot sugared almonds onto foil and let cool.

- For the salad, combine the lettuce, green onions, mandarin oranges, avocado, apple, cranberries and bleu cheese in a large bowl and mix well.

- For the dressing, combine the oil, parsley, sugar, vinegar, salt and pepper in a bowl or a jar with a tight-fitting lid and mix or shake to combine thoroughly.

- To assemble, pour the dressing over the salad and toss to coat. Top with the almonds.

- NOTE: To turn this into a one-dish meal, add 4 sliced grilled chicken breasts.

Mixed Greens with Sugared Walnuts and Balsamic Vinaigrette

MAKES 4 TO 6 SERVINGS

Balsamic Vinaigrette

1 teaspoon dry mustard
1/2 teaspoon seasoned salt
1/4 teaspoon freshly ground
 pepper
3 tablespoons balsamic
 vinegar
1/2 teaspoon grated onion
1 garlic clove, crushed
3/4 cup olive oil

Sugared Walnuts

2 tablespoons butter
1/2 cup chopped walnuts
3 tablespoons brown sugar

Salad

6 cups mixed salad greens,
 torn into bite-size pieces
1 firm pear or apple,
 chopped
1/2 cup alfalfa sprouts
 (optional)
3 green onions, sliced
3 to 4 ounces bleu cheese,
 crumbled

- FOR THE VINAIGRETTE, combine the dry mustard, seasoned salt and pepper in a bowl. Stir in the balsamic vinegar, onion and garlic. Let stand for 1 hour. Strain out the garlic and discard. Pour in the olive oil, whisking constantly. You may make this vinaigrette up to a month ahead and refrigerate. Bring to room temperature before pouring over the salad.

- For the walnuts, melt the butter in a heavy skillet over medium heat. Add the walnuts and brown sugar. Sauté until the walnuts begin to soften, stirring constantly. Remove from skillet. Let cool.

- For the salad, combine the salad greens, pear, alfalfa sprouts, green onions and half the bleu cheese in a salad bowl.

- To assemble, add half the walnuts to the salad. Drizzle with the vinaigrette. Toss to mix. Sprinkle the remaining walnuts and bleu cheese over the top. Serve immediately.

- NOTE: You may cut up the pear or apple in advance and toss it with a small amount of the vinaigrette to prevent browning.

Curried Chicken Salad

Salad

3 pounds skinless boneless
    chicken breasts
1 medium onion, cut into
    halves
1 bay leaf
6 sprigs parsley
1/2 teaspoon salt
1/4 teaspoon pepper
1 whole clove
1 cup water chestnuts, sliced
1/2 cup diagonally sliced
    green onions
Grated zest of 2 limes

Curry Dressing

1 cup mayonnaise
2 tablespoons soy sauce
Curry powder to taste
1 cup mango chutney,
    finely chopped

- FOR THE SALAD, combine the chicken, onion and enough water to cover in a large saucepan. Bring to a boil over medium-high heat. Add the bay leaf, parsley, salt, pepper and clove.

- Simmer for 25 minutes or until chicken is cooked through. Drain the chicken, discarding the water and vegetables. Let cool. Cut the chicken into bite-size pieces. Combine the chicken with the water chestnuts, green onions and lime zest in a large salad bowl.

- For the dressing, combine the mayonnaise, soy sauce, curry powder and mango chutney in a small bowl and mix well.

- To assemble, pour the dressing over the chicken mixture and mix well.

Smoked Salmon Salad

Caper Vinaigrette
1/3 cup vegetable oil
2 tablespoons red wine
   vinegar
1/2 tablespoon lemon juice
4 teaspoons drained capers
Salt and freshly ground
   pepper

Ginger
2 cups water
2 tablespoons finely
   julienned fresh ginger

Salad
4 cups loosely packed torn
   fresh spinach
1 pound smoked salmon,
   flaked

- FOR THE VINAIGRETTE, combine the oil, red wine vinegar, lemon juice, capers, salt and pepper in a bowl or a jar with a tight-fitting lid and mix well.

- For the ginger, bring the water to a boil in a small saucepan over high heat. Add the ginger and boil for 2 minutes; drain and set aside.

- For the salad, toss the spinach with half of the vinaigrette. Divide among 4 salad plates. Top with the smoked salmon. Sprinkle with the ginger. Drizzle with the remaining vinaigrette.

71

Steak and Potato Salad

Salad

3 large white all-purpose
   potatoes
3 to 4 cups sliced cooked
   steak
2/3 cup diced red and green
   bell peppers
1/3 cup chopped sweet onion
1/3 cup chopped parsley

Red Wine Aïoli

1 egg yolk
1/3 cup red wine vinegar
1 tablespoon sugar
1 tablespoon chopped garlic
Salt and pepper to taste
1 cup olive oil

- FOR THE SALAD, peel the potatoes. Scoop the potato into balls with a small melon baller. Boil the potato balls in enough water to cover in a medium saucepan until tender but not mushy; drain.

- Combine the potatoes with the steak, bell peppers, onion and parsley in a large bowl and mix well.

- For the aïoli, combine the egg yolk, red wine vinegar, sugar, garlic, salt and pepper in a food processor container fitted with a steel blade. Process briefly to mix. With the motor running, pour in the oil gradually until the mixture thickens. Adjust seasonings. Refrigerate, covered, until ready to use.

- To serve, pour the aïoli over the salad and toss to coat. Serve at room temperature.

Swan Coach House
Frozen Fruit Salad

1 cup dark sweet cherries, pitted
1 cup pineapple tidbits
1 cup diced peaches
1 cup sliced bananas
1 cup halved grapes
1 cup chopped pecans
1 quart lemon curd (or vanilla or lemon yogurt)
2 cups whipping cream

- Place fruit in a colander to drain. Whip the cream in a mixing bowl until soft peaks form. Fold in lemon curd or yogurt and add fruit and pecans. Mix well.

- Spoon the mixture into quart sized freezer containers. Freeze, covered for 8 hours or until firm.

- Unmold and slice into rounds.

Minted Peach Salad

Salad

4 large peaches, sliced, or
 1 cantaloupe, peeled
 and sliced
6 tomatoes, sliced
1/4 cup fresh mint leaves,
 chopped
2 small inner celery ribs,
 thinly sliced
1/4 teaspoon salt
1/4 teaspoon pepper

Balsamic Lemon
Dressing

1 tablespoon balsamic
 vinegar
1 tablespoon fresh lemon
 juice
1/2 teaspoon salt
1/4 teaspoon pepper
3 tablespoons olive oil

- FOR THE SALAD, arrange overlapping slices of the peaches and tomatoes on a serving platter. Sprinkle with the mint leaves and celery. Season with the salt and pepper.

- For the dressing, combine the balsamic vinegar, lemon juice, salt, pepper and olive oil in a bowl or a jar with a tight-fitting lid and mix well. Use immediately or refrigerate, covered, for up to several days. Shake or stir again just before using.

- To serve, drizzle the dressing over the salad.

Swan Coach House Bleu Cheese Dressing

MAKES ABOUT 4 CUPS

1 tablespoon dry mustard
1/2 to 2/3 cup sugar
4 teaspoons onion salt
2 teaspoons salt
1 cup apple cider vinegar
2 cups vegetable oil
1 cup crumbled bleu cheese

- COMBINE THE DRY mustard, sugar, onion salt and salt in a medium bowl and mix well. Add the vinegar and mix well. Pour in the oil, whisking vigorously. Add the bleu cheese and mix well.

Special Tarragon Mayonnaise

MAKES ABOUT 1 1/2 CUPS

1 large egg yolk
1 tablespoon Dijon mustard
1 1/2 teaspoons chopped
    fresh tarragon leaves
1 cup mild-flavored
    vegetable oil, such as
    safflower, sunflower or
    peanut oil
Juice of 1/2 large lemon
1 tablespoon ice water
Salt, pepper, cayenne
    pepper or Tabasco sauce
    to taste

- COMBINE THE EGG yolk, Dijon mustard and tarragon leaves in a food processor or blender container. Cover and pulse for a few seconds to mix. With the motor running, pour half of the oil into the blender gradually. Alternate the remaining oil with the lemon juice until both are blended in.

- Whisk in the ice water, using more if needed. Season with the salt, pepper and cayenne pepper or Tabasco sauce; mix well. Use immediately or refrigerate, covered, until ready to use.

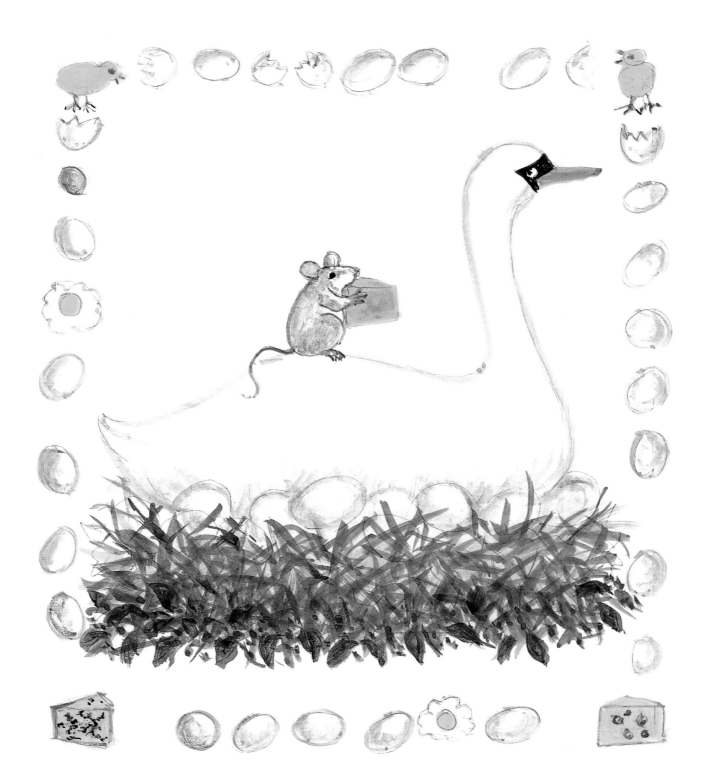

Breads and Brunch

French Toast Strata with Apple Cider Syrup

French Toast Strata

1 (1-pound) loaf French
  bread, cut into cubes
8 ounces cream cheese,
  cut into small cubes
8 eggs
2 1/2 cups milk
6 tablespoons (3/4 stick)
  butter or margarine,
  melted
1/4 cup maple syrup or
  pancake syrup

Apple Cider Syrup

1/2 teaspoon cinnamon
4 teaspoons cornstarch
1/2 cup sugar
1 tablespoon lemon juice
1 cup apple cider or
  apple juice
2 tablespoons butter or
  margarine

- FOR THE FRENCH toast strata, layer half of the bread in a greased 9x13-inch baking dish. Top with the cream cheese and the remaining bread. Blend the eggs, milk, butter and maple syrup in a blender. Pour over the bread and cream cheese. Press the layers down with a spatula. Refrigerate, covered with plastic wrap, for 2 to 24 hours.

- Bake at 325 degrees for 35 to 40 minutes or until center is set and edges are golden brown. Let stand for 10 minutes.

- For the syrup, combine the cinnamon, cornstarch and sugar in a small saucepan and mix well. Stir in the lemon juice and apple cider. Cook over medium heat until mixture thickens and boils, stirring constantly. Cook for 2 minutes longer. Remove from the heat and stir in the butter.

- To serve, cut the strata into slices and serve with the hot syrup.

- NOTE: Syrup may be made 1 day ahead and reheated before serving.

Easy Elegant Eggs

MAKES 12 SERVINGS

12 slices Canadian
   bacon or ham
12 slices Swiss cheese
12 eggs
Heavy cream or
   half-and-half
Salt and pepper to taste
Fines herbes or herbes de
   Provence to taste
Grated Parmesan cheese to
   taste

- LINE AN 9x13-INCH baking dish with Canadian bacon. Top with a layer of Swiss cheese. Break the eggs in an even pattern over the cheese. Drizzle enough cream over the egg whites until the yolks just show through. Season with salt, pepper and fines herbes.

- Bake at 450 degrees for 10 minutes. Remove the dish from the oven and sprinkle with Parmesan cheese. Bake for 10 minutes longer. Cut into serving portions.

- NOTE: You may layer well-drained, cooked spinach between the Canadian bacon and cheese for a more elaborate dish.

Mexican Breakfast Bake

MAKES 6 TO 8 SERVINGS

6 eggs, beaten
1 (4-ounce) can chopped
   green chiles, drained
1 (14-ounce) can diced
   tomatoes, drained
8 ounces shredded
   Colby-Jack cheese mixture
1 cup cottage cheese
1/4 cup (1/2 stick) butter,
   melted
1/4 cup flour
1/8 teaspoon salt

- COMBINE THE EGGS, green chiles, tomatoes, Colby-Jack cheese, cottage cheese, butter, flour and salt in a large bowl and mix well. Pour into a greased 7x11-inch baking dish.

- Bake at 375 degrees for 30 minutes or until set.

Christmas Breakfast Casserole

8 to 10 slices white bread, crusts trimmed
2 cups milk
6 eggs
16 ounces sharp Cheddar cheese, shredded
1 teaspoon dry mustard
1 pound hot bulk pork sausage, cooked and drained

- LINE A GREASED 9x13-inch baking dish with bread slices. Combine the milk, eggs, Cheddar cheese, mustard and sausage in a large bowl and mix well. Spoon over bread.

- Refrigerate, covered, for at least 8 hours. Uncover and bake at 350 degrees for 45 minutes.

Chile Cheese Omelet

10 eggs
1/2 cup flour
1 teaspoon baking powder
Generous dash of salt
1/2 cup (1 stick) butter, melted
1 (8-ounce) can chopped green chiles, drained
16 ounces cottage cheese
16 ounces shredded Monterey Jack cheese

- BEAT THE EGGS lightly in a large bowl. Add the flour, baking powder, salt, butter, green chiles, cottage cheese and Monterey Jack cheese and mix just until blended. Pour into a greased 9x13-inch baking dish.

- Bake at 400 degrees for 15 minutes. Reduce the oven temperature to 350 degrees and bake for 30 to 40 minutes longer.

Honey Whole Wheat Bread

MAKES 2 LOAVES

You may not need all of the unbleached flour that this recipe calls for. Simply add flour until the dough is no longer sticky. If you need more, add it 1 or 2 tablespoons at a time.

To shape dough into loaves simply, roll each half into a 7x14-inch rectangle. Roll as for a jelly roll, sealing the edge and ends. This bread is delicious spread with jelly or preserves for breakfast!

3 cups whole wheat flour
$1/2$ cup nonfat dry milk powder
1 tablespoon salt
2 envelopes dry yeast
$1/4$ cup wheat germ (optional)
3 cups water
$3/4$ to 1 cup honey
2 tablespoons vegetable oil
1 cup whole wheat flour
4 to $4^{1}/_{2}$ cups unbleached flour

- COMBINE THE 3 CUPS whole wheat flour, milk powder, salt, yeast and wheat germ in a large mixing bowl and mix well. Heat the water, honey and oil in a medium saucepan until warm (105 degrees to 115 degrees). Pour over the whole wheat flour mixture.

- Beat at low speed for 1 minute. Beat at medium speed for 2 minutes. Stir in the 1 cup whole wheat flour and unbleached flour with a spoon.

- Knead the dough on a floured surface for 5 minutes or until the dough is smooth and elastic. Place the dough in a greased bowl and let rise in a warm place until doubled in bulk. Punch the dough down and divide into halves. Shape each half into a loaf. Place in 2 greased loaf pans. Let rise, covered, until doubled in bulk.

- Bake at 375 degrees for 40 to 45 minutes. Cool in the pans for 5 minutes. Remove to a wire rack to cool completely before cutting.

Dill Bread

1 envelope dry yeast
1/4 cup warm water
1 tablespoon butter
1 egg
1/4 teaspoon baking soda
1 cup cottage cheese
2 tablespoons sugar
1 teaspoon salt
1 tablespoon dillseeds
1 tablespoon onion flakes
2 1/2 cups flour
Melted butter

- COMBINE THE YEAST and warm water in a large bowl. Add the butter, egg, baking soda, cottage cheese, sugar, salt, dillseeds and onion flakes and mix well. Add the flour and mix well. Let the mixture rise in the bowl until doubled in bulk. Stir or mash down. Spoon into a greased loaf pan. Let rise until doubled in bulk.

- Bake at 350 degrees for 40 to 45 minutes. To serve, slice the bread and spread the slices with melted butter. Wrap the loaf in foil and heat in a 250-degree oven until hot.

Southern Dinner Rolls

MAKES ABOUT 36 ROLLS

1 cup shortening
1 tablespoon salt
1/2 cup sugar
2 cups boiling water
2 envelopes dry yeast
1/2 cup warm water
2 eggs, beaten
7 cups flour
Vegetable oil

- COMBINE THE SHORTENING, salt, sugar and the 2 cups boiling water in a bowl and mix well. Let stand until cool.

- Dissolve the yeast in the 1/2 cup warm water in a small bowl and add to shortening mixture. Add the eggs and mix well. Add the flour 1 cup at a time and mix well.

- Grease the top of the dough, cover, and let rise in the refrigerator until doubled in bulk.

- Roll the dough on a floured surface to a 1/4-inch thickness. Cut into rounds with a 2-inch round cutter. Brush the top of each round with oil, then fold in half to form half-moons. Arrange the rolls on a baking sheet so that the edges touch.

- Bake at 400 degrees until brown. Serve hot or let cool completely on a wire rack and then freeze.

Buttery Biscuit Rolls

MAKES 24 ROLLS

1 cup (2 sticks) butter
1 cup sour cream
2 cups self-rising flour

- MELT THE BUTTER in a large saucepan over medium-low heat, whisking until completely melted. Add the sour cream and flour and mix lightly. Spoon the batter into ungreased miniature muffin cups, filling each one to the top.

- Bake at 350 degrees for 20-30 minutes, watch carefully for browning. Serve immediately. To freeze these rolls, remove them from the oven several minutes early. Cool completely, then freeze in sealable plastic bags. To serve, thaw the rolls and bake at 350 degrees for a few minutes.

- NOTE: You may add 1 tablespoon of dried herbs such as rosemary or basil, or 2 tablespoons of chopped fresh herbs, to the batter.

To measure flour properly for baking, spoon flour into a cup and level it off with a knife.

Mom's Best Biscuits

MAKES 12 BISCUITS

2 cups flour
1/2 teaspoon salt
1/2 teaspoon baking soda
4 teaspoons baking powder
4 tablespoons shortening
1 cup buttermilk

- SIFT THE FLOUR, salt, baking soda and baking powder into a bowl. Cut in the shortening with a pastry blender or 2 knives until mixture is crumbly. Add the buttermilk and stir just until blended.

- Roll the dough into a rectangle on a floured board. Cut out rounds with a biscuit cutter. Arrange on a baking sheet so the edges touch. Bake at 450 degrees for 10 to 12 minutes or until golden brown.

Broccoli Corn Bread

MAKES 10 TO 12 SERVINGS

1 cup (2 sticks) butter
1 (9-ounce) package corn muffin mix
1 (10-ounce) package frozen chopped broccoli, thawed
1 onion, chopped
16 ounces cottage cheese
4 eggs
1/2 cup shredded Cheddar cheese

- MELT THE BUTTER in a 9x13-inch baking pan in a 375-degree oven. Combine the muffin mix, undrained broccoli, onion, cottage cheese and eggs in a large bowl and mix well.

- Spoon the batter into the prepared pan and spread evenly. Sprinkle with the cheese. Bake at 375 degrees for 30 to 45 minutes or until set.

Corn Bread

MAKES 12 MUFFINS

1 cup cornmeal
1 cup bread flour
2 tablespoons sugar
1¼ teaspoons salt
1¼ teaspoons baking
  powder
2 eggs, beaten
1⅓ cups milk or buttermilk
2 tablespoons vegetable oil
  or butter

• GREASE A CAST-IRON or other muffin pan and place in a 450-degree oven until hot. Sift the cornmeal, bread flour, sugar, salt and baking powder into a bowl and mix well.

• Combine the eggs, milk and oil in a separate bowl and mix well. Add to the flour mixture and mix well. Spoon the batter into the prepared muffin pan. Bake at 450 degrees for 15 to 20 minutes.

Whole Kernel Corn Bread

MAKES 6 TO 8 SERVINGS

1 (9-ounce) package corn
  muffin mix
2 eggs, lightly beaten
6 tablespoons (3/4 stick)
  butter, melted
1 (8-ounce) can cream-style
  corn
1 (8-ounce) can whole
  kernel corn, drained
1 cup sour cream
Salt and pepper to taste

- COMBINE THE MUFFIN mix, eggs, butter, cream-style corn, whole kernel corn, sour cream, salt and pepper in a large bowl and mix well.

- Pour into an 8x8-inch baking dish. Bake at 350 degrees for 1 hour.

Bubble Bread

MAKES 24 SERVINGS

24 frozen Parker House rolls
1 cup packed light brown
  sugar
1 (5-ounce) package cook-
  and-serve butterscotch or
  vanilla pudding
1/2 cup sugar
1 teaspoon cinnamon
1/2 cup (1 stick) butter or
  margarine, melted
1 cup chopped nuts

- ARRANGE THE ROLLS in a large greased bundt pan. Sprinkle the brown sugar and pudding mix over the rolls. Mix the sugar and cinnamon in a small bowl and sprinkle over the rolls. Drizzle the butter over the rolls. Sprinkle with the nuts. Let the rolls rise for 8 hours, covered with a clean kitchen towel.

- Bake at 350 degrees for 30 to 45 minutes. Cool in the pan for 10 minutes. Remove and serve hot.

Sun-Dried Tomato and Provolone Bread

MAKES 12 SERVINGS

2 garlic cloves

2¹/₂ cups flour

2 teaspoons baking powder

1¹/₄ teaspoons salt

¹/₂ teaspoon baking soda

1 cup (about 5 ounces) shredded provolone cheese

¹/₂ cup thinly sliced scallions

2 tablespoons minced fresh parsley

³/₄ teaspoon dried rosemary

³/₄ teaspoon coarsely ground pepper

¹/₃ cup chopped drained oil-pack sun-dried tomatoes, 2 tablespoons oil reserved

2 tablespoons shortening

2 tablespoons sugar

2 eggs, beaten

1¹/₄ cups buttermilk

- BOIL THE GARLIC in enough water to cover in a small saucepan for 15 minutes; drain. Let cool. Peel the garlic and mash in a small bowl. Set aside.

- Sift the flour, baking powder, salt and baking soda into a large bowl and mix well. Add the cheese, scallions, parsley, rosemary, pepper and sun-dried tomatoes and mix well. Combine the shortening, reserved oil and sugar in a medium bowl and stir until smooth. Add the mashed garlic, eggs and buttermilk and mix well. Add to the flour mixture and stir just until combined.

- Divide the batter among 3 greased miniature loaf pans, smoothing the tops. Bake at 350 degrees for 45 to 50 minutes or until a wooden pick inserted in the center comes out clean. Cool in the pans for 5 minutes. Remove to a wire rack to cool completely.

This bread is a great start of a delicious sandwich. Layer smoked turkey and mayonnaise or champagne mustard on the bread. Perfect for cocktail parties!

Artichoke-Stuffed Bread

MAKES 15 TO 20 SERVINGS

1 (1-pound) loaf Italian or
    French bread
$1/2$ cup (1 stick) butter or
    margarine
6 garlic cloves, crushed
2 tablespoons sesame seeds
$1^1/2$ cups sour cream
2 cups shredded Monterey
    Jack cheese
$1/4$ cup grated Parmesan
    cheese
2 tablespoons parsley flakes
2 teaspoons lemon pepper
1 (14-ounce) can artichoke
    hearts, drained, chopped
1 cup shredded sharp
    Cheddar cheese

- CUT THE LOAF into halves lengthwise. Remove the bread from the center of each half, leaving a thick shell. Tear the removed bread into bite-size pieces.

- Melt the butter in a large skillet. Sauté the garlic in the butter until tender. Add the bread pieces and stir until the bread absorbs the butter.

- Combine the bread mixture, sesame seeds, sour cream, Monterey Jack cheese, Parmesan cheese, parsley, lemon pepper and artichokes in a large bowl and mix well. Mound the mixture in the bread halves. Sprinkle with the Cheddar cheese.

- Arrange the halves on foil-lined baking sheets. Bake at 350 degrees for 30 minutes. To serve, slice the halves into 2-inch pieces.

Apple Bread

MAKES 1 LOAF

1/2 cup (1 stick) butter, softened

1 cup packed brown sugar

2 eggs

1 teaspoon vanilla extract

2 teaspoons grated lemon or orange zest

2 cups flour

2 teaspoons cinnamon

1/2 teaspoon baking soda

1 teaspoon baking powder

1 teaspoon allspice

1 teaspoon nutmeg

1/2 teaspoon salt

2 tablespoons buttermilk

1 1/2 cups grated unpeeled apples

1/2 cup chopped pecans or walnuts

1/2 cup raisins or chopped dates

- CREAM THE BUTTER and brown sugar in a mixing bowl until fluffy. Beat in the eggs, vanilla and lemon zest. Sift the flour with the cinnamon, baking soda, baking powder, allspice, nutmeg and salt.

- Add the flour mixture to the egg mixture alternately with the buttermilk, beginning and ending with the flour mixture. Stir in the apples, pecans and raisins.

- Pour the batter into a greased loaf pan. Tap the pan or rap on the counter to release any air bubbles. Bake at 350 degrees for 1 hour or until a wooden pick inserted in the center comes out clean.

- NOTE: You may substitute 2/3 cup sugar and 1/4 cup honey for the brown sugar.

Holiday Cranberry Bread

MAKES 1 LOAF

2 cups flour
1 cup sugar
1 1/2 teaspoons baking
    powder
1/2 teaspoon baking soda
1/2 teaspoon salt
3/4 cup orange juice
2 tablespoons vegetable oil
1 egg
1 cup cranberries

- SIFT THE FLOUR, sugar, baking powder, baking soda and salt into a large bowl and mix well. Combine the orange juice, oil and egg in a small bowl and mix well. Add to the flour mixture and stir just until combined. Stir in the cranberries.

- Spoon the batter into a greased loaf pan. Bake at 350 degrees for 1 hour to 1 hour and 10 minutes or until a wooden pick inserted in the center comes out clean.

- NOTE: If possible use fresh orange juice in this recipe.

Lemon Blueberry Loaf with Streusel

MAKES 1 LARGE LOAF

Bread

2¹/₂ cups flour
¹/₄ cup cornmeal
1 tablespoon baking powder
1 teaspoon salt
1¹/₂ cups sugar
³/₄ cup (1¹/₂ sticks) butter,
   melted
3 eggs
¹/₂ cup milk
1 tablespoon lemon zest
2 tablespoons lemon juice
1 cup blueberries
1 tablespoon flour

Streusel

¹/₂ cup flour
2 tablespoons sugar
2 tablespoons brown sugar
¹/₄ teaspoon cinnamon
¹/₄ cup (¹/₂ stick) butter, cut
   into pieces

- FOR THE BREAD, combine the 2¹/₂ cups flour, cornmeal, baking powder, salt and sugar in a large bowl and mix well. Combine the butter, eggs, milk, lemon zest and lemon juice in a medium bowl and mix well. Add to the flour mixture and stir just until combined. Toss the blueberries with 1 tablespoon flour until coated. Stir into the batter. Pour the batter into a large greased loaf pan.

- For the streusel, combine the flour, sugar, brown sugar and cinnamon in a medium bowl. Cut in the butter with a pastry blender or 2 knives until mixture is crumbly. Sprinkle over the loaf. Bake at 350 degrees for 50 minutes.

- NOTE: You may use 5 miniature loaf pans instead of 1 large loaf pan and reduce the baking time to 30 to 35 minutes or until the loaves test done. May store, covered, in the freezer.

Orange Poppy Seed Bread

MAKES 2 LOAVES

Bread

3 cups flour
2 1/4 cups sugar
2 tablespoons poppy seeds
1 1/2 teaspoons baking
   powder
1/2 teaspoon salt
3 eggs
1 1/2 cups milk
1 cup vegetable oil
2 tablespoons grated
   orange zest
1 teaspoon vanilla extract
1/2 teaspoon almond extract

Orange Glaze

3/4 cup sifted confectioners'
   sugar
1/4 cup orange juice
1/2 teaspoon vanilla extract
1/2 teaspoon almond extract

- FOR THE BREAD, combine the flour, sugar, poppy seeds, baking powder and salt in a large mixing bowl and mix well. Combine the eggs, milk, oil, orange zest, vanilla and almond extract in a medium bowl and mix well. Add to the flour mixture and beat for 2 minutes.

- Pour the batter into 2 greased loaf pans. Bake at 350 degrees for 1 hour or until a wooden pick inserted in the center comes out clean.

- For the glaze, combine the confectioners' sugar, orange juice, vanilla and almond extract in a medium bowl and mix well.

- To assemble, poke holes in the loaves with a long-tined fork. Pour the glaze over the loaves. Cool in the pans for 10 minutes. Remove to a wire rack to cool completely.

French Breakfast Muffins

Muffins

1 1/2 cups plus 2 tablespoons
   flour
3/4 cup sugar
2 teaspoons baking powder
1/4 teaspoon salt
1/4 teaspoon nutmeg
1/2 cup milk
1 egg, beaten
1/3 cup butter, melted

Cinnamon Topping

3/4 cup sugar
1/2 teaspoon vanilla extract
1 teaspoon cinnamon

Assembly

3/4 cup (1 1/2 sticks) butter,
   melted

- FOR THE MUFFINS, combine the flour, sugar, baking powder, salt and nutmeg in a large bowl and mix well. Combine the milk, egg and butter in a small bowl and mix well. Add to the flour mixture and stir just until combined. Spoon the batter into 12 greased and floured muffin cups. Bake at 400 degrees for 20 minutes.

- For the topping, combine the sugar, vanilla and cinnamon in a small bowl; mix well.

- To assemble, remove the hot muffins from the cups and roll in the melted butter and then in the topping.

- NOTE: If you prefer, you may use miniature muffin cups. Bake for 10 to 15 minutes or until muffins test done. You may need extra butter for rolling the hot muffins.

Entrées

Beef Bourguignon

MAKES 20 SERVINGS

Use fresh white pearl onions. To peel them, cut an X in the root end. Boil them in enough water to cover in a saucepan for 5 minutes, drain, and run under cool water. Peels will slip off easily. Frozen pearl onions may also be used; they are already peeled.

10 pounds beef chuck, cut into 1 1/2-inch pieces
2 cups flour
4 1/2 teaspoons salt
1 1/2 teaspoons pepper
1/2 cup (1 stick) butter
1/2 cup olive oil
3/4 cup Cognac
1 pound bacon, diced
6 garlic cloves, minced
8 carrots, chopped
4 leeks, chopped
4 yellow onions, chopped
1/4 cup chopped fresh parsley
3 bay leaves
1 1/2 teaspoons thyme
1/4 cup tomato paste
7 cups burgundy wine
6 cups beef broth
50 to 60 small white onions (see sidebar)
1/2 cup (1 stick) butter
2 tablespoons sugar
3 pounds small fresh mushrooms, stemmed
1/2 cup (1 stick) butter
Juice of 1 lemon
1/2 cup chopped fresh parsley
Salt and pepper to taste

- COAT THE BEEF with the flour mixed with 4 1/2 teaspoons salt and 1 1/2 teaspoons pepper. Heat 1/2 cup butter and olive oil in a heavy skillet and brown the beef in batches. Add more butter and oil if needed. Drain the beef and arrange in two or three 2 1/2-quart heavy ovenproof casserole dishes.

- Warm the Cognac in a saucepan over low heat or in a glass cup in the microwave. Pour it into the skillet and ignite. Stir vigorously to scrape up the brown bits on the bottom of the skillet. Pour over the beef in the casserole.

- Cook the bacon, garlic, carrots, leeks, yellow onions and 1/4 cup parsley until bacon is crisp. Add the bay leaves, thyme and tomato paste; mix well. Pour over the beef. Add the burgundy and enough broth to barely cover; mix well. Bake, covered, at 350 degrees for 2 hours, stirring occasionally and adding broth as needed.

- Peel the small white onions. Sauté in the 1/2 cup butter with the sugar in a large skillet, shaking the pan occasionally. Cook until browned and caramelized. Add enough broth to the skillet to barely cover the onions. Cook, covered, for 15 minutes.

- Sauté the mushrooms in the 1/2 cup butter in a skillet until tender. Add the lemon juice and 1/2 cup parsley. Add the mushrooms and onions to the beef. Cook for 1 hour longer. Remove the bay leaves. Skim the surface. Season with salt and pepper to taste.

London Broil with Pineapple Salsa

Bourbon Marinade

2 garlic cloves, crushed
Pinch of salt
1/2 cup Dijon mustard
1/3 cup bourbon
1/4 cup packed brown sugar
1 small onion, thinly sliced
1/4 cup lemon juice
3/4 cup plain yogurt
2 tablespoons olive oil

Steak

4 pounds flank steak

Pineapple Salsa

1 large pineapple
1/2 cup loosely packed fresh
   mint leaves, chopped
1/4 cup sugar
2 tablespoons white vinegar

- FOR THE MARINADE, mash the garlic with salt until a paste forms. Combine the paste with the mustard, bourbon, brown sugar, onion, lemon juice, yogurt and olive oil in a large bowl and mix well.

- For the steak, add the flank steak to the marinade, turning to coat. Refrigerate, covered, for 4 hours or longer.

- For the salsa, peel the pineapple and cut out the eyes. Cut the pineapple into small chunks. Combine with the mint, sugar and vinegar in a medium bowl and mix well. Let stand, covered, for 1 hour or longer.

- To prepare, grill or broil the steak for 10 minutes on each side or until a meat thermometer reaches 130 degrees. Let stand for 10 minutes. Slice thinly on the diagonal against the grain. Serve the steak with the salsa.

For **Beef Marinade** to tenderize flank steak or sirloin, combine 1 part Worcestershire sauce, 1 1/2 parts soy sauce, 1/2 part vegetable oil, plus rosemary and garlic powder to taste. Marinate the beef, covered, in a shallow dish in the refrigerator for 4 hours or longer.

Country-Fried Steak

Béarnaise Sauce
is the classic accompaniment to filet mignon, but it can also dress up any steak, including pan-fried minute steaks or sirloin burgers. This blender version is simple and speedy.

Combine 2 tablespoons white wine, 1 tablespoon tarragon vinegar, $1/2$ teaspoon dried tarragon, $1/4$ teaspoon pepper and 2 teaspoons chopped green onions in a small saucepan. Bring to a boil over medium-high heat. Boil until only a spoonful of liquid remains. Set aside.

(continued on page 103)

$1^{1}/_{2}$ cups flour
$1/_{8}$ teaspoon white pepper
12 minute steaks
Vegetable oil for frying
2 (10-ounce) cans cream of
    mushroom soup
2 tablespoons
    Worcestershire sauce
2 tablespoons soy sauce
2 cups milk
1 (10-ounce) can beef broth
$1/_{4}$ teaspoon garlic powder
3 small onions, sliced
    (optional)

- COMBINE THE FLOUR and white pepper in a shallow dish or sealable plastic storage bag and mix well. Coat the steaks with the flour mixture. Refrigerate, covered, for 30 minutes.

- Fry the steaks in hot oil in a large skillet in batches until brown. Drain and set the steaks aside.

- Heat the mushroom soup in a saucepan over medium heat, stirring until smooth. Stir in the Worcestershire sauce and soy sauce, milk, beef broth, garlic powder and onions and mix well.

- Arrange the steaks in a Dutch oven or casserole dish. Pour the mushroom soup mixture over the steaks. Bake at 300 degrees for 1 hour.

- NOTE: If you prefer a thin gravy, add additional milk and broth to the mushroom soup mixture.

Beef Stew with Fennel and Pecans

MAKES 8 TO 10 SERVINGS

Stew

3 pounds sirloin tip or
   chuck roast
3 tablespoons bacon
   drippings or olive oil
2 medium onions, sliced
1/4 cup flour
1/2 cup dry white wine
2 tablespoons chopped
   fresh rosemary, or
   1 tablespoon dried
   rosemary
1 tablespoon chopped
   fresh thyme
2 garlic cloves, minced
Juice and zest of 1 lemon
1 tablespoon fennel seeds
2 1/2 cups beef broth
Salt and pepper to taste

Fennel Pecan Topping

1/4 cup (1/2 stick) butter
2 fennel bulbs, sliced, cored
2 cups toasted pecan halves

Assembly

Hot cooked noodles
Zest of 1 orange

- FOR THE STEW, cut the beef into 2-inch cubes. Heat the drippings in a heavy ovenproof casserole dish or Dutch oven over medium heat. Brown the beef in batches until deep brown on all sides. Remove from pan. Add the onions to the pan and cook just until they begin to brown. Drain all but 1/4 cup of the drippings. Add the flour to the pan and mix well. Add the wine and mix well. Cook until mixture boils, stirring constantly. Add the browned beef, rosemary, thyme, garlic, lemon zest, lemon juice and fennel seeds to the pan. Add enough broth to cover the beef. Stir the mixture, cover and cook over low heat for 1 1/2 hours or until tender.

- Skim the stew with paper towels or place several ice cubes in the stew and then skim out with a spoon, or refrigerate, covered, until chilled and then skim the surface. Stew may be frozen at this point.

- Reheat the stew by bringing to a boil over low heat. Simmer for 10 minutes.

- For the topping, melt the butter in a large skillet. Add the fennel slices and sauté for a few minutes. Stir in the pecans. The topping may be made up to 4 hours in advance and reheated, but for best flavor prepare no more than 10 minutes in advance.

- To assemble, ladle the stew into bowls over hot cooked noodles. Spoon the topping over the stew and sprinkle with orange zest.

Béarnaise Sauce
(continued)

Combine the 3 egg yolks, 2 tablespoons lemon juice, 1/4 teaspoon salt and a pinch of red pepper in a blender container. Process at low speed. Remove the lid immediately. Slowly pour 1/2 cup (1 stick) melted butter into the blender container until all the butter is used. Turn off the blender. Add the white wine mixture and blend for a few seconds. Makes about 3/4 cup.

Shepherd's Pie

For **Mashed Potatoes**, boil 2 pounds quartered peeled potatoes in 1 quart water in a covered pan until tender. Drain well. Return to pan. Add 5 tablespoons butter, 1 teaspoon salt and $1/3$ cup warm milk or cream and mash thoroughly. Makes 6 to 8 servings.

1 pound ground beef
1 teaspoon thyme
1 bay leaf
1 large onion, sliced
8 ounces carrots, finely chopped
2 teaspoons cornstarch
$1^1/4$ cups water
1 beef bouillon cube
Salt and pepper to taste
2 teaspoons steak sauce
2 dashes of Tabasco sauce
$1/4$ cup peas
Mashed Potatoes (at left)

- BROWN THE GROUND beef with the thyme and bay leaf in a large saucepan. Add the onion and carrots and cook for 5 minutes, stirring occasionally.

- Dissolve the cornstarch in $1/4$ cup of the water in a small saucepan. Add the remaining 1 cup water and the bouillon cube. Bring to a boil, stirring occasionally. Pour over the ground beef mixture and mix well. Simmer for 20 minutes.

- Add the salt, pepper, steak sauce and Tabasco sauce to the ground beef mixture and mix well. Scatter the peas over the bottom of a 9x11-inch baking dish. Cover with the ground beef mixture and then a thick layer of Mashed Potatoes. Bake at 375 degrees for 30 minutes or until browned and bubbly.

Oscar's Meat Loaf

1 pound ground round or
  veal
1/2 pound sage-flavored bulk
  pork sausage
1 carrot, finely chopped
2 ribs celery, finely chopped
1 1/2 onions, finely chopped
1 egg
3/4 cup bread crumbs
1 small garlic clove, minced
2 tablespoons fresh parsley,
  chopped
1/2 green bell pepper,
  chopped
2 teaspoons Worcestershire
  sauce (optional)
Salt and pepper to taste
1 1/2 cups canned tomatoes
1/2 cup water

• COMBINE THE GROUND round, sausage, carrot, celery, onions, egg, bread crumbs, garlic, parsley, bell pepper, Worcestershire sauce, salt and pepper in a large bowl and mix well. Form into a loaf in a loaf pan or a baking dish. Pour a mixture of the tomatoes and water over the loaf.

• Bake, covered, at 350 degrees for 3 hours. Uncover the loaf pan near the end of the cooking process to allow the top to brown.

Picadillo

2 medium onions, chopped
1 large green bell pepper, chopped
2 garlic cloves, minced
2 tablespoons olive oil
1 1/2 pounds ground chuck
2 tablespoons olive oil
1/3 teaspoon celery salt
1/4 teaspoon salt
1/4 teaspoon pepper
1/4 teaspoon paprika
1 (29-ounce) can tomato sauce
1 tablespoon Worcestershire sauce
1 (10-ounce) jar pimento-stuffed olives
1 (3-ounce) jar capers, drained
1 cup white raisins
1/4 cup dry sherry or red wine

- SAUTÉ THE ONIONS, bell pepper and garlic in the 2 tablespoons olive oil in a large skillet. Remove from the skillet with a slotted spoon. Add the ground chuck. Cook until brown, stirring to crumble; drain.

- Drain the olives, reserving 1/4 cup of the liquid. Add the 2 tablespoons olive oil to the skillet. Stir in the reserved olive liquid, celery salt, salt, pepper, paprika, tomato sauce, Worcestershire sauce, olives, capers and raisins. Add the onion mixture and mix well.

- Cook, covered, over low heat for 40 minutes. Add the wine. Cook, covered, until the flavors are blended. Serve over hot cooked rice. For a Cuban specialty, top with a fried egg.

Corned Beef Po' Boys

3 cups finely chopped
   cabbage
3/4 cup finely chopped celery
1 tablespoon grated onion
1/4 cup mayonnaise
1 teaspoon salt
1/3 teaspoon red pepper
   flakes
1 small garlic clove, minced
4 large hoagie rolls
Softened butter
Mustard
12 ounces corned beef,
   sliced
Sliced tomatoes
Lettuce leaves

- COMBINE THE CABBAGE, celery, onion, mayonnaise, salt, red pepper flakes, and garlic in a medium bowl and mix well. Refrigerate, covered, for 1 hour or longer.

- When ready to serve, split the rolls and spread with butter. Toast the rolls, then spread with mustard. Warm the corned beef. Layer the corned beef, cabbage mixture, tomatoes and lettuce on the rolls. Press down top of roll to compress layers.

Mint-Barbecued Leg of Lamb

MAKES 10 TO 12 SERVINGS

Lamb

1 (5-pound) boneless leg of
   lamb
1 teaspoon salt
1 garlic clove, cut into
   8 slices

Mint Sauce

1/2 cup mint jelly
1 tablespoon butter
1 teaspoon grated
   lemon zest
1 tablespoon lemon juice
1/2 teaspoon salt
1/2 cup cider vinegar
1/4 cup packed light
   brown sugar
1/4 cup sugar
1/2 teaspoon dry mustard

- FOR THE LAMB, flatten the lamb to a uniform 2-inch thickness. Score the skin side of the lamb in a crisscross fashion. Wipe the lamb with a damp cloth. Sprinkle with the salt. Make slashes in the meat and insert slivers of garlic. Place the lamb in a large shallow baking dish.

- For the sauce, combine the mint jelly, butter, lemon zest, lemon juice, salt, cider vinegar, brown sugar, sugar and dry mustard in a small saucepan and mix well. Cook over low heat until the jelly is melted, stirring constantly. Bring to a boil. Let cool and pour over the lamb. Let stand for 30 minutes, turning once. Remove the lamb, reserving the sauce.

- Pour the reserved sauce into a small saucepan. Bring to a boil. Cook for several minutes or until heated through, stirring frequently.

- Adjust the grill rack 5 inches from the prepared coals or turn a gas grill to medium-high heat. Grill the lamb for 20 to 30 minutes, turning and basting several times with some of the reserved sauce. Begin testing for doneness after 20 minutes. Grill to desired taste. Serve with any remaining sauce.

Veal Forestier

2 pounds very thin
   veal cutlets
1 garlic clove, or garlic
   powder to taste
Flour for coating
1/4 to 1/2 cup (1/2 to 1 stick)
   butter
1/2 to 3/4 pound thinly
   sliced mushrooms
Salt and seasoned pepper
   to taste
1/3 cup dry vermouth
1 teaspoon fresh lemon
   juice
2 tablespoons chopped
   fresh parsley

- POUND THE VEAL very thin with a wooden mallet. Rub all over with a cut garlic clove or sprinkle with garlic powder. Coat the veal with flour.

- Heat the butter in a large skillet over medium-high heat. Sauté the veal until golden brown on both sides, adding more butter to the skillet if needed. Heap mushrooms on each piece of veal and sprinkle with salt, pepper and vermouth.

- Cook, covered, over very low heat for 20 minutes. Add water if necessary to keep the veal moist. Just before serving, sprinkle with lemon juice and parsley.

- NOTE: You may substitute thin turkey cutlets if you prefer. May store the cooked veal, covered, in the freezer.

Veal Giardino

Tomato Vinaigrette

1 medium garlic clove, crushed
1 tablespoon balsamic vinegar
3 tablespoons olive oil
Salt and pepper to taste
1/4 small red onion, sliced paper-thin
2 medium tomatoes, chopped

Salad

1 cup packed watercress
1 medium Belgian endive, or 1 cup fresh field greens, torn into bite-size pieces

Veal

2 ounces grated Parmesan cheese
1 1/2 cups dry bread crumbs
1/8 teaspoon nutmeg
1 1/2 teaspoons white pepper
2 eggs
1/4 cup vegetable oil
1/4 cup olive oil
1 pound veal scallops, pounded thin

- FOR THE VINAIGRETTE, combine the garlic, vinegar, olive oil, salt, pepper, onion and tomatoes in a bowl and mix well. Let stand at room temperature for at least 30 minutes before serving. Remove the garlic before serving.

- For the salad, combine the watercress and endive in a large bowl and mix well. Cover with a clean kitchen towel. Chill, covered, in the refrigerator.

- For the veal, combine the Parmesan cheese, bread crumbs, nutmeg and white pepper in a bowl and mix well. Spread on a platter or plate. Beat the eggs lightly in a small bowl. Combine the vegetable oil and olive oil in a separate bowl. Dip each veal scallop into the egg, then coat thoroughly with crumbs, pressing so crumbs adhere.

- Heat 3 tablespoons of the oil mixture in a large skillet over medium-high heat. Sauté the veal in batches until cooked through. Place the cooked veal onto a paper towel-lined baking sheet and place in a 250-degree oven to keep warm.

- To assemble, toss the salad with the vinaigrette. Divide the veal among 4 serving plates. Top with a heaping cup of salad. Serve immediately.

Marinated Pork Tenderloin

MAKES 4 SERVINGS

Lime Marinade

6 garlic cloves
6 ounces frozen limeade
   concentrate, thawed
1/4 cup soy sauce
1 teaspoon salt
1 tablespoon pepper

Pork Tenderloins

2 to 3 pounds pork
   tenderloins

Assembly

1 tablespoon flour
1/2 cup red wine

- FOR THE MARINADE, combine the garlic, limeade concentrate, soy sauce, salt and pepper in a bowl or shallow dish.

- For the pork, add the tenderloins to the bowl and marinate, covered, in the refrigerator for at least 3 hours and up to 24 hours.

- Remove the pork from the marinade and reserve the marinade. Grill the tenderloins until they are just slightly pink in the middle, about 140 to 150 degrees, turning frequently.

- To assemble, bring the reserved marinade to a boil in a saucepan over high heat. Boil until reduced by half. Whisk in the flour and red wine. Bring to a boil. Sauce should be of a syrupy consistency. Serve with sliced pork tenderloin.

- NOTE: You may bake the tenderloins at 400 degrees for 20 minutes. Reduce the oven temperature to 325 degrees and bake for 30 minutes longer, turning frequently.

Texas Indonesian Pork

3 pounds pork loin
3/4 teaspoon salt
Pepper to taste
1 tablespoon ground
  coriander
2 tablespoons vegetable oil
1/4 cup chopped shallots
1 tablespoon brown sugar
1/4 cup soy sauce
Dash of ground ginger
Juice of 3 limes
1 tablespoon cumin
Chutney
Hot cooked rice

- CUT THE PORK into 1 1/2-inch cubes. Combine the pork, salt, pepper, coriander and oil in a large bowl and stir to coat. Let stand for 20 minutes. Add the shallots, brown sugar, soy sauce, ginger, lime juice and cumin to the bowl and mix well. Refrigerate, covered, for at least 1 hour and up to 10 hours.

- Remove the pork and the marinade to an ovenproof dish. Broil for 30 minutes or until cooked through, stirring occasionally. Serve with chutney and hot cooked rice.

- NOTE: You may arrange the pork on skewers, alternating with fresh mushrooms, then broil for about 15 minutes.

Pork Tenderloin with Balsamic Raisin Sauce

1/4 cup olive oil
3 pork tenderloins
1 small onion, minced
6 shallots, minced
2 garlic cloves, minced
Balsamic Raisin Sauce
     (at right)
1 tablespoon balsamic
     vinegar
3 tablespoons unsalted
     butter
Salt and pepper to taste

- HEAT THE OLIVE oil in a large heavy ovenproof skillet over medium-high heat. Add the pork tenderloins and cook for 3 minutes or until brown on 1 side. Add the onion and shallots and cook for 12 to 15 minutes or until the pork is brown on all sides and the onion is tender. Stir in the garlic.

- Place the skillet in a 450-degree oven and bake for 15 to 20 minutes or until a meat thermometer inserted in the thickest part of the pork registers 140 degrees. Place the pork on a platter and tent with foil to keep warm.

- Add the Balsamic Raisin Sauce to the skillet and bring to a boil. Boil, scraping up any brown bits from the bottom. Add the balsamic vinegar. Remove from the heat and whisk in the butter. Season with salt and pepper. Keep the sauce warm.

- Slice the pork into 1/2-inch-thick slices. Arrange the slices overlapping slightly on a serving platter. Surround with Garlicky Oven-Roasted Vegetables (page 179). Pour the sauce over the pork.

For **Balsamic Raisin Sauce,** combine 1/2 cup raisins and 1 cup dry red wine in a small bowl. Let stand for 8 hours. Pour into a small heavy saucepan and add 3 tablespoons dark brown sugar and 1 tablespoon balsamic vinegar. Bring the mixture to a boil. Boil for 7 minutes or until the liquid is reduced to 1 tablespoon. Stir in 1 1/2 cups chicken broth or stock. Boil until the mixture is reduced by half. You may prepare the sauce up to 2 days ahead. Refrigerate, covered, until ready to use.

Oven-Glazed Spareribs

1 cup cider vinegar
$^1/_2$ cup ketchup
2 tablespoons sugar
2 tablespoons
   Worcestershire sauce
1 teaspoon salt
1 teaspoon dry mustard
1 teaspoon paprika
$^1/_8$ teaspoon pepper
1 garlic clove, minced
2 to 2$^1/_2$ pounds spareribs

- COMBINE THE VINEGAR, ketchup, sugar, Worcestershire sauce, salt, dry mustard, paprika, pepper and garlic in a saucepan and mix well. Bring to a boil over medium-high heat. Reduce heat to low and simmer for 10 minutes.

- Trim any excess fat from the ribs. Arrange the ribs in a large pan and bake at 500 degrees for 10 to 15 minutes. Reduce the oven temperature to 325 degrees. Brush the ribs with the sauce. Bake for 30 minutes.

- Turn the ribs and brush with the sauce again and bake for 30 minutes longer. Turn the ribs again and brush with the sauce. Bake, covered with foil, for 30 minutes or until tender and cooked through. Serve the ribs with any remaining sauce.

Chicken Country Captain

Flour for coating
Salt and pepper to taste
2¹/₂ to 3 pounds chicken
   pieces
2 tablespoons vegetable oil
2 tablespoons (or more)
   butter
1 onion, sliced
1 large green bell pepper,
   sliced
1 or 2 garlic cloves, crushed
2 (15-ounce) cans whole
   tomatoes
1 teaspoon salt
1 teaspoon curry powder
1 teaspoon thyme
1 teaspoon dried parsley
¹/₂ teaspoon white pepper
4 ounces blanched sliced
   almonds, toasted
2 tablespoon dried currants
   or raisins
Hot cooked rice
Chopped fresh parsley

- COMBINE THE FLOUR and salt and pepper to taste in a shallow dish and mix well. Coat the chicken with the flour mixture. Heat the oil and 2 tablespoons butter in a large skillet. Add the chicken and cook until brown on all sides, turning occasionally. Arrange the chicken in a baking dish.

- Add 1 tablespoon additional butter to the skillet if needed. Sauté the onion, bell pepper and garlic in the butter until the onion is tender. Add the tomatoes. Bring to a boil and simmer for 10 minutes. Add the salt, curry powder, thyme, 1 teaspoon parsley and white pepper and cook for 5 minutes longer, stirring occasionally. Pour the tomato mixture over the chicken.

- Bake, tightly covered, at 350 degrees for 45 minutes or until the chicken is tender. Remove the chicken to a serving platter. Stir the almonds and currants into the sauce and pour over the chicken. Surround with hot cooked rice and garnish with chopped fresh parsley.

All-Season Barbecued Chicken

For **Daddy's Famous Barbecue Sauce,** combine 2 cups ketchup, 6 cups vinegar, 1/4 cup A.1. steak sauce, 1/4 cup Heinz 57 Steak Sauce, 1/2 cup Worcestershire sauce, 1/2 cup hot red pepper sauce, 2 tablespoons lemon juice, 2 tablespoons onion juice, 1 tablespoon garlic juice, 2 tablespoons sugar, 1 tablespoon salt, 1 tablespoon cayenne pepper and 1 tablespoon dry mustard in a large saucepan and mix well. Bring to a boil over medium heat. Reduce the heat to low and simmer for 45 minutes. Pour into clean jars with tight-fitting lids. You may store the sauce at room temperature for several weeks.

Barbecue Sauce
2 teaspoons salt
1/4 teaspoon pepper
1 1/2 cups tomato juice
1/4 teaspoon cayenne pepper
1/4 teaspoon dry mustard
1 bay leaf
4 1/2 teaspoons Worcestershire sauce
3/4 cup cider vinegar
1 teaspoon sugar
3 garlic cloves, minced
3 tablespoons butter

Chicken
1 chicken, cut up, or 6 chicken breasts
Salt and pepper to taste
2 onions, thinly sliced

- FOR THE SAUCE, combine the salt, pepper, tomato juice, cayenne pepper, dry mustard, bay leaf, Worcestershire sauce, vinegar, sugar, garlic and butter in a saucepan and mix well. Bring to a boil over medium heat. Simmer for 10 minutes. Discard the bay leaf.

- For the chicken, arrange the chicken skin side down in a large baking dish. Season with salt and pepper. Cover with the onions.

- Bake at 425 degrees for 30 minutes, basting occasionally with the sauce. Reduce the oven temperature to 350 degrees, turn, and bake for 45 minutes longer, basting occasionally. Remove the chicken to a serving platter. Pour the remaining sauce over the chicken.

Sweet and Mild Barbecued Chicken

MAKES 6 TO 8 SERVINGS

Sweet and Mild Barbecue Sauce

4 tablespoons mustard
2/3 cup packed brown sugar
1 cup water
1 cup vinegar
1 medium onion, sliced
1 lemon, thinly sliced
1 garlic clove, minced
2 (12-ounce) bottles
  chili sauce
1/4 cup (1/2 stick) butter
2 tablespoons
  Worcestershire sauce
1/4 cup corn syrup
Dash of cayenne pepper

Chicken

2 chickens, quartered

- FOR THE SAUCE, combine the mustard, brown sugar, water, vinegar and onion in a saucepan. Add the lemon slices and garlic to the saucepan. Bring to a boil, reduce the heat to low, and simmer for 15 minutes or until the mixture has reduced somewhat in volume.

- Add the chili sauce, butter, Worcestershire sauce, corn syrup and cayenne pepper and mix well. Return to a boil. Simmer until the mixture is thickened.

- For the chicken, combine the chicken quarters with a small amount of the sauce in a large bowl or sealable plastic bag, reserving the remaining sauce. Refrigerate, covered, for 1 hour or longer.

- Remove the chicken to a large flat baking pan. Bake at 325 degrees for 25 minutes. Place the chicken on a hot grill and grill until chicken is cooked through, basting with the reserved sauce.

Chicken Chasseur

1/4 cup flour
1 tablespoon salt
1/4 teaspoon pepper
1/4 teaspoon basil or
    oregano
2 1/2 pounds chicken pieces
    or 6 boneless skinless
    chicken breasts
3 tablespoons butter or
    olive oil
4 sliced green onions
4 ounces sliced mushrooms
2 tablespoons lemon juice
1 teaspoon sugar
1/3 cup white wine
2 medium ripe tomatoes
Hot cooked rice

- COMBINE THE FLOUR, salt, pepper and basil in a shallow dish and mix well. Coat the chicken with the flour mixture.

- Heat the butter in a large skillet over medium heat. Add the chicken to the skillet and cook until brown on all sides. Add the green onions and mushrooms to the skillet. Simmer, covered, for 3 minutes or until the mushrooms are tender. Stir in the lemon juice, sugar and wine. Simmer, covered, for 5 minutes.

- Add the tomatoes. Simmer, covered, for 30 minutes, checking occasionally to ensure that the chicken is not sticking. Serve the chicken and sauce over hot cooked rice.

Chicken Tortilla Casserole

1 (10-ounce) can cream of
  mushroom soup
1 (10-ounce) can cream of
  chicken soup
1 cup sour cream
1 (6-ounce) can sliced black
  olives (optional)
1 onion, chopped
1 (10-ounce) can diced
  tomatoes and green
  chilies
1 (15-ounce) can black
  beans, rinsed and
  drained
1 (15-ounce) can corn,
  drained (optional)
2 dashes of Tabasco sauce
6 large flour tortillas,
  cut into strips
5 boneless chicken breasts,
  cooked and cut into
  pieces
10 ounces sharp Cheddar
  cheese, shredded

- COMBINE THE CREAM of mushroom soup, cream of chicken soup and the sour cream in a medium bowl and mix well. Add the olives, onion, tomatoes, black beans, corn and Tabasco sauce and mix well.

- Spread a small amount of the mixture over the bottom of a 3-quart baking dish. Arrange a layer of tortilla strips over the sauce, then a layer of chicken over the tortilla strips. Top with a layer of the soup mixture then a layer of cheese. Repeat the layers until all the ingredients are used.

- Bake, covered, at 350 degrees for 45 minutes or until bubbly.

Chicken Cheese Casserole

MAKES 6 SERVINGS

You can make your own **Homemade Stuffing.** Just measure 1 cup of chunky dry bread crumbs. Arrange the bread crumbs on a baking sheet and bake until toasted. Combine the toasted bread crumbs with a small amount of Mrs. Dash, sage and thyme and use them as the recipe directs.

6 small chicken breast halves
6 slices Swiss cheese
1 (10-ounce) can cream of mushroom soup
1/4 cup white wine
1 (8-ounce) package herb-seasoned stuffing mix or Homemade Stuffing (at left)
1/4 cup (1/2 stick) butter, melted

- ARRANGE THE CHICKEN in a greased baking dish. Place 1 slice of cheese on each piece of chicken.

- Combine the cream of mushroom soup and wine in a small bowl and mix well. Spoon over the chicken and cheese. Sprinkle the stuffing mix over the top. Drizzle with the butter. Bake, covered, at 350 degrees for 45 minutes.

Chicken Vegetable Stir-Fry

MAKES 6 SERVINGS

1 tablespoon cornstarch
1 cup chicken broth
3 tablespoons dry sherry
2 tablespoons soy sauce
1/2 teaspoon hot pepper
    sauce
1/4 cup peanut oil
3 chicken breasts, skinned,
    deboned, and cut into
    bite-size pieces
1 teaspoon grated fresh
    ginger
3 cups broccoli florets
1 red bell pepper, cut into
    1-inch squares
8 ounces sliced mushrooms
1 bunch green onions,
    thinly sliced
1 garlic clove, minced
1/2 cup dry-roasted cashews
Hot cooked rice

- COMBINE THE CORNSTARCH, chicken broth, sherry, soy sauce and hot pepper sauce in a small bowl and mix well.

- Heat the peanut oil in a heavy skillet over high heat. Add the chicken and ginger. Cook until the chicken turns opaque, stirring constantly. Remove from the skillet. Add the broccoli, bell pepper, mushrooms, green onions and garlic. Cook for 3 minutes, stirring constantly.

- Combine the chicken with the cornstarch mixture and add to the skillet. Cook until the mixture thickens and boils, stirring constantly. Remove to a serving platter. Sprinkle with cashews. Serve immediately with hot cooked rice.

Indian Chicken Curry

4 slices bacon, chopped
1/3 cup chopped celery
1/3 cup chopped onion
1 garlic clove, minced
2 tablespoons vegetable oil
1/4 cup flour
2 chicken bouillon cubes
1 1/4 cups boiling water
1/2 cup applesauce
1/4 cup good-quality curry
  powder, preferably
  Madras
3 tablespoons tomato paste
1 tablespoon sugar
1 tablespoon lemon juice
Salt to taste
2 cups light cream
2 whole chicken breasts,
  cooked, chopped
Hot cooked rice
Shredded coconut, peanuts,
  chopped green onions,
  onion slices, chutney,
  raisins, cubed cantaloupe
  and/or sliced kiwifruit

- SAUTÉ THE BACON, celery, onion and garlic in the oil in a large skillet for about 10 minutes. Sprinkle with the flour and cook over very low heat for 5 minutes.

- Dissolve the bouillon cubes in the boiling water in a small bowl. Add to the skillet with the applesauce, curry powder, tomato paste, sugar, lemon juice and salt. Cook, covered, over low heat for 45 minutes.

- Let cool. Refrigerate, covered, for 8 hours or longer. Reheat over low heat. Add the cream and chicken and mix well. Cook until heated through.

- Serve over hot cooked rice and offer bowls of garnishes, including shredded coconut, peanuts, green onions, onion slices, chutney, raisins, cubed cantaloupe and/or sliced kiwifruit.

Chicken Florentine with Sherry Artichoke Sauce

Chicken

8 ounces spaghetti
2 garlic cloves, minced
2 tablespoons butter
2 (10-ounce) packages
    frozen chopped spinach,
    thawed, drained
4 cups chopped cooked
    chicken

Sherry Artichoke Sauce

1 pound fresh mushrooms,
    sliced
8 tablespoons butter
1/2 cup sliced green onions
1/2 cup flour
2 tablespoons chopped
    fresh parsley
1/2 teaspoon salt
1/2 teaspoon pepper
2 cups milk
3 ounces shredded Swiss
    cheese
Zest of 1 lemon
2 tablespoons fresh
    lemon juice
3/4 cup dry white wine
1/4 cup dry sherry
2 (8-ounce) cans artichoke
    hearts, drained, chopped

- FOR THE CHICKEN, break the spaghetti into thirds and cook according to package directions. Sauté the garlic in 2 tablespoons butter in a small skillet. Toss the cooked spaghetti with the garlic butter and place in a greased 3-quart baking dish. Layer the spinach over the spaghetti. Layer the chicken over the spinach.

- For the sauce, sauté the mushrooms in 3 tablespoons of the butter in a skillet until tender. Set aside. Melt the remaining 5 tablespoons butter in a large skillet. Add the green onions and cook until tender. Stir in the flour, parsley, salt and pepper. Add the milk gradually.

- Cook until just thickened, stirring constantly. Remove from the heat. Add the cheese and stir until the cheese melts. Add the lemon zest, lemon juice, wine, sherry, artichoke hearts and mushrooms.

- To assemble, pour the sauce over the chicken. Bake at 350 degrees for 30 to 40 minutes or until bubbly.

- NOTE: You may freeze the casserole before baking.

Chicken Enchiladas

MAKES 4 SERVINGS

Enchilada Sauce

3 tablespoons flour
1 tablespoon chili powder
$1/2$ teaspoon paprika
$1/4$ teaspoon cumin
$1/2$ teaspoon oregano
Pinch of thyme
Pinch of pepper
$1/4$ teaspoon garlic granules
$2^1/2$ cups vegetable stock
1 tablespoon chopped fresh
  cilantro
1 teaspoon honey
1 teaspoon lime juice
1 teaspoon salt

Chicken Filling

$1/2$ cup minced onion
12 ounces diced cooked
  chicken breasts
1 teaspoon oregano
1 teaspoon chili powder
$1/2$ cup vegetable stock

Assembly

8 corn tortillas
8 teaspoons sour cream
8 ounces shredded reduced-
  fat Cheddar cheese
4 ounces shredded lettuce

- FOR THE SAUCE, combine the flour, chili powder, paprika, cumin, oregano, thyme, pepper and garlic in a large skillet. Cook over medium heat until brown, stirring frequently. Whisk in the vegetable stock, cilantro, honey, lime juice and salt. Bring to a boil and reduce heat to low. Simmer for 45 minutes, stirring often to prevent scorching.

- For the filling, sauté the onion, chicken, oregano and chili powder in a skillet coated with cooking spray until chicken is brown. Add the vegetable stock and simmer until the liquid has evaporated.

- To assemble, soak each tortilla briefly in warm water. Lay on a flat work surface and spoon 3 tablespoons of the chicken mixture and 1 teaspoon sour cream down the right side of each tortilla. Roll tightly to enclose the filling.

- Arrange the filled tortillas in an 8-inch square baking pan. Ladle the sauce over the top and sprinkle with Cheddar cheese. Bake at 350 degrees for 15 minutes or until the cheese is melted and the sauce is bubbly. Garnish with lettuce.

Hot Chicken Salad

4 cups chopped cooked
 chicken, chilled
3/4 cup mayonnaise
1 teaspoon salt
1 cup shredded Cheddar
 cheese
4 hard-cooked eggs,
 finely chopped
1 teaspoon chopped onion
2 tablespoons lemon juice
2/3 cup toasted almonds,
 chopped
2 cups chopped celery
1/2 (10-ounce) can cream of
 chicken soup
2 whole pimentos, chopped
1 cup crushed potato chips

- COMBINE THE CHICKEN, mayonnaise, salt, cheese, eggs, onion, lemon juice, almonds, celery, cream of chicken soup and pimentos in a large bowl and mix well. Spread in a greased 9x13-inch baking dish. Top with crushed potato chips.

- Refrigerate, covered, for at least 8 hours. Bake at 400 degrees for 25 to 30 minutes. Serve hot.

Smothered Quail

MAKES 4 TO 6 SERVINGS

6 tablespoons (³/₄ stick)
   butter
6 quail, cleaned, rinsed,
   patted dry
3 tablespoons flour
¹/₂ cup dry sherry
2 cups chicken broth
Salt and pepper to taste
Hot cooked rice

- HEAT THE BUTTER in a large skillet over medium heat. Add the quail to the skillet and cook until brown. Remove the quail from the skillet. Arrange in a baking dish. Add the flour to the skillet. Cook until all the butter is absorbed, stirring constantly. Add the sherry, chicken broth, salt and pepper and mix well.

- Pour the sherry mixture over the quail. Bake, covered, at 350 degrees for 1 hour. Serve with hot cooked rice.

- NOTE: You may substitute an equivalent amount of chicken for the quail.

Leasel's Southern Dove

MAKES 2 OR 3 SERVINGS

Dove
6 dove, cleaned
Salt and pepper to taste
Flour for coating
6 tablespoons (3/4 stick)
    butter
1 (10-ounce) can beef broth
2 cups hot water

Brown Sugar Glaze
6 tablespoons
    Worcestershire sauce
1/4 cup vinegar
1 tablespoon A.1. Steak
    Sauce
3 tablespoons brown sugar
1 teaspoon dry mustard
Salt and pepper to taste

Assembly
Celery ribs
Sliced onion
Flour for thickening
Wild Rice (at right)

- FOR THE DOVE, season the dove with salt and pepper. Coat with flour. Brown in hot butter in a large skillet; drain excess drippings. Place the dove in a roaster with a lid or an ovenproof casserole dish. Pour the beef broth over the dove. Add enough water to cover. Cook, covered, over low heat for 1 hour; drain most of the liquid.

- For the glaze, combine the Worcestershire sauce, vinegar, A.1. Sauce, brown sugar, dry mustard and salt and pepper to taste in a saucepan and mix well. Add 2 cups hot water and mix well.

- To assemble, pour the glaze over the dove. Top with enough celery ribs and onion slices to cover. Bake, covered, at 350 degrees for 1 to 1 1/2 hours or until the dove are very tender.

- Remove the dove to a serving platter, reserving the pan drippings. Pour the pan drippings into a saucepan. Whisk in 1 tablespoon of flour for every cup of liquid. Cook over medium heat until thickened, stirring constantly. Serve the dove with the sauce and Wild Rice.

For **Wild Rice,** combine 1 cup wild rice with enough water to cover in a saucepan. Bring to a boil. Boil for 10 minutes. Drain thoroughly. Repeat this procedure a total of 5 times. On the last boiling, add salt to taste to the water.

Salmon with French Lentils

MAKES 6 SERVINGS

French Lentils

1/2 cup julienned bacon or
　　Canadian bacon
2 tablespoons olive oil
1/2 cup minced shallots
1/2 cup chopped carrots
1/2 cup chopped celery
1 cup dry red wine
2 cups French lentils
6 cups chicken stock
2 tablespoons chopped
　　fresh thyme
2 tablespoons chopped
　　fresh chives
1 teaspoon butter
Salt and freshly ground
　　pepper to taste

Salmon

6 (6-ounce) salmon fillets
2 tablespoons olive oil
1/4 cup lemon juice
2 tablespoons butter
Salt and freshly ground
　　pepper to taste

- FOR THE LENTILS, sauté the bacon in the olive oil in a medium saucepan over medium heat. Add the shallots, carrots and celery to the pan and cook until the shallots are tender. Add the red wine and simmer until all the liquid has evaporated.

- Add the lentils, chicken stock and thyme. Simmer over medium-low heat for 45 minutes or until the lentils are tender. Add the chives, butter, salt and pepper.

- For the salmon, sauté the salmon in the olive oil in a large skillet for 6 minutes. Turn and cook for 1 minute longer or until the salmon is just medium-rare. Add the lemon juice and butter to the pan. Season with salt and pepper.

- To serve, divide the lentils among 6 serving plates. Top with a salmon fillet. Drizzle lemon butter pan juices over each serving.

Grilled Sea Bass with Cilantro Lime Butter

Cilantro Lime Butter

1¹/₂ tablespoons unsalted
  butter, softened
1 teaspoon freshly grated
  lime zest
1 teaspoon fresh lime juice
1 small garlic clove, minced
1 tablespoon minced fresh
  cilantro
Salt and pepper to taste

Sea Bass

2 (6- to 8-ounce) sea bass
  steaks
2 teaspoons fresh lime juice
Salt and pepper to taste

- FOR THE BUTTER, combine the butter, lime zest, lime juice, garlic, cilantro, salt and pepper in a small bowl and mix well.

- For the sea bass, rub the steaks with the lime juice and sprinkle with salt and pepper. Grill in a ridged pan over medium-high heat for 5 minutes or until fish flakes easily, turning once.

- To serve, top each steak with a small amount of the Cilantro Lime Butter.

- NOTE: The Cilantro Lime Butter is also a nice accompaniment to grilled chicken.

Spiced Grilled Swordfish with Tomato Compote

Tomato Compote

1 pound fresh tomatoes
1 tablespoon olive oil
1 garlic clove, crushed
2 teaspoons red wine
    vinegar

Spicy Dry Rub

1 teaspoon salt
$1/2$ teaspoon pepper
$1/2$ teaspoon cumin
$1/4$ teaspoon paprika
$1/4$ teaspoon celery salt
$1/4$ teaspoon garlic powder
$1/8$ teaspoon nutmeg

Swordfish

2 (8-ounce) swordfish steaks
Olive oil

- FOR THE COMPOTE, peel, seed and chop the tomatoes. Heat the olive oil in a medium skillet over high heat. Add the tomatoes and garlic and cook for 2 minutes or until the tomatoes soften. Remove from the heat and stir in the vinegar. Let cool to room temperature.

- For the dry rub, combine the salt, pepper, cumin, paprika, celery salt, garlic powder and nutmeg in a bowl or on waxed paper.

- For the swordfish, brush the swordfish with olive oil. Sprinkle $3/4$ teaspoon of the dry rub on each side of the swordfish. Grill for 4 minutes per side or until the swordfish flakes easily and is opaque in the center.

- To serve, spoon the tomato compote over the swordfish.

Grilled Tuna with Mango Papaya Relish

Mango Papaya Relish

1 mango, peeled, seeded, chopped
1 papaya, peeled, seeded, chopped
1 tablespoon chopped fresh cilantro
2 tablespoons lemon juice
Salt and pepper to taste

Tuna

4 tuna steaks
1 teaspoon ground coriander
1 tablespoon olive oil
Salt and pepper to taste

- FOR THE RELISH, purée half of the mango, half of the papaya and the cilantro in a blender or food processor. Transfer to a bowl. Add the remaining mango and papaya and the lemon juice, salt and pepper to the bowl and mix well.

- For the tuna, rub the tuna with the olive oil and sprinkle with the coriander, salt and pepper. Grill for 4 to 5 minutes per side for medium-rare. Serve with the relish.

- NOTE: You may make the relish several hours in advance and store, covered, in the refrigerator.

Steamed Mussels

2 pounds mussels
1 cup white wine
3 shallots, minced
3 garlic cloves, minced
1 teaspoon butter
2 tablespoons minced fresh
  thyme
2 tablespoons minced fresh
  parsley
1/2 cup cream (optional)
Salt and pepper to taste
Hot cooked pasta

- SCRUB THE MUSSELS and remove the beards. Discard any mussels that are open. Combine the mussels, wine, shallots, garlic, butter, thyme and parsley in a large saucepan. Cook over high heat, covered, for 5 to 7 minutes or until the mussels open. Discard any mussels that do not open.

- Remove the mussels from the liquid with a slotted spoon, add the cream and boil for 2 to 3 minutes. Season with salt and pepper. Mound the hot cooked pasta in a large bowl. Surround with mussels. Spoon the sauce over the mussels.

- NOTE: You may also serve this dish as an appetizer, omitting the pasta.

Crab Cakes with Basil Sauce

Basil Sauce

1/2 cup fresh basil, rinsed in
   hot water and patted dry
1/4 cup mayonnaise
1/4 cup sour cream
1 teaspoon lemon juice
1/2 teaspoon minced garlic
Dash of red pepper

Crab Cakes

2 eggs
1/4 to 1/2 cup mayonnaise
1 teaspoon lemon juice
1/2 teaspoon Worcestershire
   sauce
1/2 teaspoon red pepper
1/2 teaspoon dry mustard
2 tablespoons sliced
   green onions
2 tablespoons bread crumbs
1 pound lump crab meat,
   rinsed, drained
Bread crumbs for coating
3 tablespoons vegetable oil
3 tablespoons butter

- FOR THE SAUCE, combine the basil, mayonnaise, sour cream, lemon juice, garlic and red pepper in a blender or food processor container and process until blended. Refrigerate, covered, until serving time.

- For the crab cakes, combine the eggs, mayonnaise, lemon juice, Worcestershire sauce, red pepper, dry mustard and green onions in a bowl and mix well. Add the bread crumbs and crab meat and mix well.

- Divide the mixture into 8 equal portions and shape into patties. Coat the patties with bread crumbs. Sauté in a mixture of the oil and butter in a large skillet for 10 minutes, turning once.

- To assemble, place 2 crab cakes on each plate and serve with the sauce.

- NOTE: You may prepare the crab mixture several hours in advance. Refrigerate, covered, until ready to prepare the dish.

Crab Meat Mornay

1/2 cup (1 stick) butter
1 small bunch green onions,
    sliced
1/2 cup finely chopped fresh
    parsley
2 tablespoons flour
2 cups half-and-half
8 ounces shredded
    Swiss cheese
1 tablespoon sherry
Salt and red pepper to taste
1 pound lump crab meat

- MELT THE BUTTER in a heavy pan and sauté the green onions and parsley until tender. Add the flour, half-and-half and cheese and cook until the cheese melts, stirring frequently. Add the sherry, salt, red pepper and crab meat and mix gently.

- Serve in patty shells, as a sauce for fish fillets, or as an appetizer in a chafing dish with melba toast.

Easy Grilled Scallops and Shrimp

MAKES **4** SERVINGS

1 pound fresh sea scallops
2 pounds fresh large shrimp,
    peeled and deveined
2 to 3 tablespoons olive oil
Tony Chachere's Cajun/
    Creole Seasoning
    to taste
Chef Paul Prudhomme's
    Seafood Magic Seasoning
    to taste

- RINSE AND DRAIN the scallops and place in a bowl. Add the shrimp. Drizzle with the olive oil and sprinkle with seasonings to taste. Toss to coat. Skewer the seafood, beginning and ending with the shrimp. Grill on an oiled grill rack for 2 minutes per side or just until cooked through.

Grilled Shrimp with Black Bean and Mango Salsa

Black Bean and Mango Salsa

3 (15-ounce) cans black beans, drained
1/2 teaspoon salt
2 garlic cloves, minced
2 mangoes, peeled and chopped
1 red bell pepper, chopped
1 red onion, chopped

Cilantro Dressing

1/4 cup chopped fresh cilantro
1 tablespoon cumin
1 tablespoon chili powder
2 tablespoons olive oil
1/2 cup fresh lime juice

Shrimp

2 pounds medium shrimp, peeled and deveined

Assembly

Shredded lettuce

- FOR THE SALSA, combine the beans, salt, garlic, mangoes, bell pepper and onion in a large bowl and mix well.

- For the dressing, combine the cilantro, cumin, chili powder, olive oil and lime juice in a bowl or a jar with a tight-fitting lid and mix or shake to blend.

- For the shrimp, grill the shrimp in a fish basket or on skewers for 6 minutes or until opaque, turning once.

- To assemble, combine the dressing with the salsa and shrimp and mix well. Serve on a platter lined with shredded lettuce.

- NOTE: To take along as a potluck dish, keep the shrimp, salsa and dressing separate until ready to serve.

Glazed Baked Shrimp

MAKES 4 SERVINGS

1 cup (2 sticks) butter
1 cup vegetable oil
2 teaspoons minced garlic
4 bay leaves, finely
    crumbled
2 teaspoons rosemary,
    crushed
1/2 teaspoon basil
1/2 teaspoon oregano
1/2 teaspoon salt
1/2 teaspoon cayenne
    pepper
1 tablespoon paprika
3/4 teaspoon freshly ground
    black pepper
1 tablespoon lemon juice
2 pounds fresh shrimp,
    unpeeled

- MELT THE BUTTER with the oil in a medium saucepan or ovenproof casserole dish. Add the garlic, bay leaves, rosemary, basil, oregano, salt, cayenne pepper, paprika, black pepper and lemon juice and mix well.

- Cook over medium heat until the mixture comes to a boil, stirring constantly. Reduce the heat to low and simmer for 7 to 8 minutes, stirring frequently. Remove from the heat and add the shrimp. Return the mixture to a boil. Cook for 6 to 8 minutes or until the shrimp turn pink.

- Place the pan in a preheated 450-degree oven. Bake for 10 minutes. Spoon the shrimp into serving bowls. Stir the sauce and ladle over the shrimp.

- NOTE: Eat the shrimp with your hands, providing spoons for the sauce and plenty of napkins.

Shrimp Creole

Creole Sauce

2 tablespoons unsalted
    butter
1 cup julienned onion
1 cup julienned green bell
    pepper
2 ribs celery, julienned
2 garlic cloves, thinly sliced
1 bay leaf
2 tablespoons paprika
2 cups diced fresh tomatoes
1 cup tomato juice
4 teaspoons Worcestershire
    sauce
4 teaspoons Tabasco sauce
1 1/2 tablespoons cornstarch
1/2 cup water

Shrimp

1/4 cup (1/2 stick) unsalted
    butter
3 pounds fresh peeled
    shrimp

Assembly

Hot cooked rice

- FOR THE SAUCE, melt the butter in a sauté pan and add the onion, bell pepper, celery, garlic and bay leaf. Sauté for 1 to 2 minutes. Add the paprika before the onion is translucent. Add the tomatoes and tomato juice and mix well. Add the Worcestershire sauce and Tabasco sauce and simmer until reduced by a fourth and the vegetables are tender.

- Combine the cornstarch and water in a small bowl and mix well. Stir into the tomato mixture and cook for 2 minutes or until mixture thickens, stirring constantly. Discard the bay leaf.

- For the shrimp, melt the butter in a skillet. Add the shrimp. Sauté for 5 minutes or until the shrimp turn pink, stirring constantly.

- To assemble, pour the sauce over the shrimp and mix well. Serve with hot cooked rice.

Shrimp and Rice Casserole

MAKES 6 SERVINGS

3 pounds shrimp, cooked,
  peeled, deveined
1 cup rice, cooked
  according to package
  directions
1 cup shredded sharp
  Cheddar cheese
1 (10-ounce) can cream of
  mushroom soup
1/2 cup (1 stick) butter
1/2 cup chopped green
  bell pepper
1/2 cup sliced green onions
1/2 cup chopped celery
Thinly sliced lemons

- COMBINE THE SHRIMP, rice, cheese and cream of mushroom soup in a bowl and mix well. Heat the butter in a sauté pan. Add the bell pepper, green onions and celery and cook until tender. Add to the shrimp mixture and mix well.

- Spoon into a 9x13-inch baking dish. Cover completely with sliced lemons. Bake, covered, at 375 degrees for 30 minutes.

- NOTE: You may store this dish, covered, in the freezer after baking.

Curried Shrimp Casserole

MAKES 8 SERVINGS

1¹/₂ cups uncooked rice
1 medium onion, grated
³/₄ cup (1¹/₂ sticks) butter
1¹/₂ teaspoons curry powder
1 teaspoon ground
    white pepper
1 teaspoon celery salt
2¹/₂ pounds shrimp, cooked,
    peeled, deveined
¹/₂ cup slivered almonds
³/₄ cup raisins
Salt and pepper to taste
6 slices bacon, cooked and
    crumbled

- COOK THE RICE in a saucepan according to package directions. Set aside.

- Sauté the onion in the butter in a large skillet until translucent. Add the curry powder, pepper and celery salt and mix well. Add the rice and shrimp and mix well. Stir in the almonds and raisins. Season with salt and pepper. Spoon the mixture into a 2-quart baking dish.

- Bake at 350 degrees for 20 minutes or until heated through. Top with the bacon just before serving.

- NOTE: You may substitute an equivalent amount of chicken for the shrimp.

Low Country Boil

For the easiest seafood boil dinner, cover an inexpensive table with newspaper, or brown paper. Place large platters of the boiled food on the table and let guests simply place shrimp shells and corn cobs on the paper. When the time comes to clean up, just roll up the paper and discard. For traditional accompaniments to a seafood boil, see the recipe for Classic Cocktail Sauce (at right) and Easy Rémoulade Sauce (page 141).

6 bay leaves
Salt and pepper to taste
1 1/2 to 2 pounds smoked
   sausage, cut into 2-inch
   lengths
12 to 15 new red potatoes
8 to 12 ears fresh corn,
   shucked
3 1/4 to 4 pounds fresh,
   unpeeled shrimp

- FILL A LARGE stockpot with water and add the bay leaves, salt and pepper. Bring to a boil over high heat. Add the sausage and potatoes and boil for 30 minutes. Cut or break the corn into halves and add to the stockpot. Boil for 10 minutes. Add the shrimp and boil for 3 to 5 minutes or until the shrimp turn pink; drain.

- Serve immediately with Classic Cocktail Sauce (below), Easy Rémoulade Sauce (page 141) or other seafood sauce.

Classic Cocktail Sauce

1/2 cup chili sauce
1/2 cup ketchup
Juice of 1 lemon
1 1/2 teaspoons
   Worcestershire sauce
1 tablespoon horseradish,
   or to taste

- COMBINE THE CHILI sauce, ketchup, lemon juice, Worcestershire sauce and horseradish in a small bowl and mix well. Chill, covered, until serving time.

Easy Rémoulade Sauce

MAKES 1¾ CUPS

1 cup mayonnaise
1 tablespoon finely chopped
  onion
1 tablespoon finely chopped
  celery
1 tablespoon chopped fresh
  parsley
2 tablespoons Dijon mustard
1 tablespoon prepared
  horseradish
1 teaspoon paprika
½ teaspoon salt
Dash of Tabasco sauce
¼ cup vegetable oil
1 tablespoon vinegar
½ teaspoon Worcestershire
  sauce

• COMBINE THE MAYONNAISE, onion, celery, parsley, Dijon mustard, horseradish, paprika, salt, Tabasco sauce, oil, vinegar and Worcestershire sauce in a bowl and mix well. Chill, covered, in the refrigerator until serving time.

Classic Italian Lasagna

MAKES 8 SERVINGS

1½ pounds Italian sausage
2 yellow onions, chopped
2 small garlic cloves, minced
2 (16-ounce) cans Italian
  plum tomatoes, chopped
1 (4-ounce) can tomato
  paste
½ cup vermouth
1 teaspoon basil
1 teaspoon oregano
½ cup fresh parsley,
  chopped
½ teaspoon sugar
Salt and pepper to taste
½ cup grated Parmesan
  cheese
8 ounces fresh mushrooms,
  sliced
2 tablespoons butter
1 pound ricotta cheese
2 eggs, beaten
1 (8-ounce) package
  lasagna noodles, cooked
  and drained
2 cups shredded mozzarella
  cheese

- COOK THE SAUSAGE with the onions and garlic in a large skillet over medium heat, stirring until crumbly; drain. Add the tomatoes, tomato paste, vermouth, basil, oregano, parsley, sugar, salt, pepper and Parmesan cheese to the skillet and mix well. Reduce the heat and simmer for 30 minutes.

- Sauté the mushrooms in the butter in a small skillet over high heat until tender; add to the sauce. Combine the ricotta cheese and eggs in a bowl and mix well.

- Layer the sauce, noodles, ricotta cheese mixture and mozzarella cheese ½ at a time in a large rectangular baking dish, ending with the mozzarella cheese.

- Bake at 375 degrees for 30 minutes or until hot and bubbly. Let stand for 20 minutes before serving.

Vegetable Lasagna

3 cups sliced zucchini

2 cups (about 8 ounces) sliced mushrooms

1 cup chopped onion

3 garlic cloves, minced

1 tablespoon olive oil

1 (26-ounce) jar tomato and basil pasta sauce

1 teaspoon oregano

16 ounces nonfat cottage cheese

1 cup grated Parmesan cheese

1 (16-ounce) package lasagna noodles

2 cups shredded reduced-fat mozzarella cheese

1/4 cup chopped fresh parsley, or 2 tablespoons dried parsley

- SAUTÉ THE ZUCCHINI, mushrooms, onion and garlic in the olive oil in a large skillet over high heat until tender. Add the pasta sauce and oregano and mix well. Reduce the heat and simmer for 15 minutes.

- Combine the cottage cheese and Parmesan cheese in a bowl and mix well.

- Layer the uncooked noodles, sauce, cottage cheese mixture and mozzarella cheese 1/2 at a time in a large rectangular baking dish, ending with the mozzarella cheese. Sprinkle the parsley over the top.

- Bake, covered, at 350 degrees for 45 minutes. Uncover and bake for 15 minutes longer. Let stand for 20 minutes before serving.

Two Hearts Chicken and Pasta

MAKES 6 SERVINGS

12 ounces sliced mushrooms
Olive oil for sautéing
1 bunch green onions, white
    part only, chopped
3/4 tablespoon minced garlic
    (about 3 large cloves)
3 skinless boneless chicken
    breast halves, cut into
    bite-size pieces
1/2 teaspoon basil
1/2 teaspoon thyme
1 1/2 teaspoons dried parsley
1/4 cup lemon juice
2 (14-ounce) cans fat-free,
    reduced-sodium chicken
    broth
1 (15-ounce) can water-
    pack artichoke heart
    quarters, drained
1 (15-ounce) can water-
    pack hearts of palm,
    drained, cut into 1/4-inch
    rounds
3 tablespoons drained,
    chopped, oil-packed
    sun-dried tomatoes
Salt and pepper to taste
1 pound penne pasta
Freshly grated Parmesan
    cheese

- SAUTÉ THE MUSHROOMS in a small amount of olive oil in a large skillet until tender. Remove and set aside. Sauté the green onions and garlic in a small amount of olive oil in the skillet until tender. Remove and set aside.

- Sauté the chicken in a small amount of olive oil in the skillet until brown. Add the basil, thyme, parsley, mushrooms, green onions and garlic to the skillet and mix well. Add the lemon juice and chicken broth.

- Simmer for 10 to 15 minutes or until the chicken is cooked through. Add the artichoke hearts, hearts of palm and sun-dried tomatoes to the skillet. Simmer for about 10 minutes. Season with the salt and pepper. Refrigerate, covered, for 8 to 12 hours for best results.

- Prepare penne pasta according to package directions; drain. Place the cooked pasta in a large baking dish. Pour the chicken mixture over the top and mix thoroughly. Bake, covered, at 350 degrees until hot and bubbly. Top with Parmesan cheese.

Noodles with Smoked Salmon and Dill Sauce

MAKES **4** FIRST-COURSE SERVINGS

Dill Sauce

3 tablespoons minced
shallots
1/2 cup dry white wine
1 cup heavy cream
2 tablespoons chopped fresh
dillweed

Noodles

8 ounces fresh egg noodles,
or 6 ounces dried egg
noodles

Assemby

4 ounces thinly sliced
smoked salmon, cut
along the grain into
3/8x2-inch strips
Salt and pepper to taste

- FOR THE SAUCE, combine the shallots and white wine in a saucepan. Bring to a boil. Reduce the heat and simmer until the wine is reduced to about 2 teaspoons. Stir in the cream. Bring the mixture to a boil and simmer for 5 minutes. Remove from the heat. Stir in the dillweed.

- For the noodles, cook the noodles in boiling salted water according to package directions until al dente. Rinse and drain. Place the noodles in a large serving bowl.

- To assemble, pour the dill sauce over the noodles in the bowl and toss to coat. Stir in the salmon gently. Season with salt and pepper.

Salmon and Dill Bowties

MAKES 8 SERVINGS

1 pound bowtie or other
  medium-small pasta
1¹/₂ pounds cooked salmon,
  skinned, deboned, flaked
¹/₄ cup chopped fresh dill
3 celery ribs, chopped
1 medium onion, chopped
¹/₄ cup vegetable oil
2 tablespoons lemon juice
1 tablespoon white wine
  vinegar
Pepper to taste

- COOK THE PASTA according to package directions; drain. Combine with the salmon in a large bowl. Add the dill, celery and onion and mix gently. Whisk the oil, lemon juice and white wine vinegar in a bowl. Pour over the salmon. Season with pepper and toss to mix. Refrigerate, covered, until ready to serve.

Penne with
Scallop Tomato Basil Sauce

MAKES 4 SERVINGS

8 large tomatoes
4 garlic cloves, minced
¹/₃ cup olive oil
1 teaspoon salt
¹/₂ teaspoon crushed red
  pepper
1 pound penne pasta
1 pound scallops
¹/₂ cup fresh basil leaves,
  chopped
2 tablespoons chopped fresh
  flat-leaf parsley
¹/₄ cup grated Parmesan
  cheese

- PEEL, SEED AND coarsely chop the tomatoes. Sauté the garlic in the olive oil in a large skillet until golden brown. Add the tomatoes, salt and red pepper. Simmer for 5 minutes.

- Cook the pasta for 7 minutes or until just barely tender; drain. Add to the tomato mixture and mix well.

- Slice the scallops into ¹/₄-inch rounds. Add to the sauce with the basil and parsley and mix well. Cover and remove from the heat. Let stand for 5 minutes to cook the scallops. Uncover and top with the Parmesan cheese.

Pasta with Chardonnay Shrimp Sauce

1 cup sliced mushrooms
1 tablespoon olive oil
1 pound medium shrimp, peeled and deveined
1 1/2 cups chardonnay
2 tablespoons minced shallots
2 tomatoes, peeled and diced
3/4 cup heavy cream
1 pound angel hair pasta
1/4 cup heavy cream
3 tablespoons chopped parsley

- SAUTÉ THE MUSHROOMS in the olive oil in a medium saucepan. Cook until the liquid evaporates. Remove from the pan and set aside. Combine the shrimp and chardonnay in the saucepan. Cook over medium-low heat until the liquid boils. Remove the shrimp with a slotted spoon.

- Add the shallots and tomatoes to the liquid and boil for 5 minutes or until reduced to about 1/2 cup. Add the 3/4 cup cream and boil until thickened, stirring frequently. Add the shrimp and mushrooms and cook until heated through.

- Prepare the angel hair pasta according to package directions; drain. In a bowl, toss the pasta with the 1/4 cup cream and parsley. Divide the pasta among 4 serving plates. Top with the shrimp sauce.

Garlicky Ginger Shrimp on Angel Hair Pasta

MAKES 2 SERVINGS

2 garlic cloves, minced
1 (1-inch) piece ginger,
  peeled and grated
2 tablespoons peanut oil
8 ounces fresh shrimp,
  peeled
1 (8-ounce) can sliced water
  chestnuts, drained
1 carrot, shredded
1/2 green bell pepper, cut
  into julienne strips
1/2 red bell pepper, cut into
  julienne strips
3 to 4 tablespoons soy
  sauce
4 ounces angel hair pasta
Chopped cilantro

- SAUTÉ THE GARLIC and ginger in the peanut oil in a large skillet over medium-high heat until golden brown. Add the shrimp and sauté until opaque. Stir in the water chestnuts, carrot and bell peppers. Add the soy sauce and mix well. Stir-fry until the vegetables are tender-crisp and heated through.

- Prepare the angel hair pasta according to package directions; drain. Place the pasta in a large serving bowl. Spoon the shrimp mixture over the pasta. Sprinkle with cilantro.

Herbed Shrimp and Feta Pasta Bake

MAKES 12 SERVINGS

2 large eggs
1 cup evaporated milk
1 cup plain yogurt
8 ounces feta cheese,
  crumbled
5 ounces shredded Swiss
  cheese
1/3 cup fresh parsley,
  chopped
1 teaspoon basil
1 teaspoon oregano
4 garlic cloves, minced
8 ounces angel hair pasta
1 (16-ounce) jar chunky
  salsa
2 pounds fresh shrimp,
  peeled and deveined
8 ounces shredded
  mozzarella cheese

- COMBINE THE EGGS with the milk, yogurt, feta cheese, Swiss cheese, parsley, basil, oregano and garlic in a medium bowl and mix well.

- Prepare the angel hair pasta according to package directions; drain.

- Layer 1/2 of the pasta, the salsa and 1/2 of the shrimp in a greased 8x12-inch baking dish. Top with the remaining pasta. Pour the egg mixture over the pasta. Arrange the remaining shrimp over the top. Sprinkle with the mozzarella cheese. Bake at 350 degrees for 30 minutes.

Pasta Florentine

16 ounces rigati

2 medium zucchini, thinly sliced

2 red bell peppers, cut into strips

1 pound mushrooms, sliced

1 cup sliced green onions

1/4 cup (1/2 stick) butter or olive oil

2 cups chopped tomatoes

1/2 cup flour

2 cups milk

1 (14-ounce) can chicken or vegetable broth

1/2 teaspoon nutmeg

1/4 teaspoon pepper

2 (10-ounce) packages frozen chopped spinach, thawed, drained

1/2 cup grated Parmesan cheese

- COOK THE RIGATI according to package directions for 7 minutes; drain. Divide the pasta between 2 greased 9x13-inch baking dishes. Sauté the zucchini, bell peppers, mushrooms and green onions in the butter in a skillet for 3 to 4 minutes or until tender-crisp. Add the tomatoes and cook for 5 minutes. Spoon the vegetables over the pasta, reserving the drippings in the skillet.

- Whisk the flour into the reserved pan drippings. Add the milk and whisk until smooth. Add the chicken broth, nutmeg and pepper. Cook until thickened, whisking constantly. Add the spinach and Parmesan cheese and mix well. Pour over the vegetables. Bake, covered, at 350 degrees for 40 minutes or until heated through.

- NOTE: You may prepare this recipe 1 day in advance before baking and store, covered, in the refrigerator. Bring to room temperature and bake as directed. May also bake and store, covered, in the freezer until ready to serve.

Herbed Lemon Pasta

MAKES **4** SERVINGS

Pasta

2 quarts water
Juice of 1 lemon
1 tablespoon salt
1 tablespoon olive oil
8 ounces fettuccini or
   linguini

Lemon Sauce

1 large garlic clove, minced
1/4 cup chopped fresh basil,
   or 2 teaspoons dried basil
2 tablespoons butter
2 tablespoons olive oil
Grated zest and juice of
   1 medium lemon
1/4 cup chopped fresh
   parsley (preferably
   flat-leaf)
1/3 cup grated Parmesan
   cheese
Salt and freshly ground
   pepper to taste

Assembly

1/3 cup grated Parmesan
   cheese
Chopped fresh parsley

- FOR THE PASTA, bring the water to a boil in a large saucepan. Add the lemon juice, salt and olive oil to the water. Add the fettuccini. Cook for 8 to 10 minutes or until tender; drain.

- For the sauce, sauté the garlic and basil in the butter and olive oil in a skillet for 2 to 3 minutes. Stir in the lemon zest and lemon juice. Reduce the heat to low. Add the parsley, Parmesan cheese, salt and pepper and mix well.

- To assemble, place the pasta in a large serving bowl and toss with the sauce. Sprinkle the Parmesan cheese over the top. Garnish with additional parsley.

Tortellini with Sun-Dried Tomatoes and Pepperoni

MAKES **6** SERVINGS

4 ounces thinly sliced
  pepperoni
2 garlic cloves, minced
1 cup drained, oil-packed,
  sun-dried tomatoes
1 tablespoon Dijon or green
  peppercorn mustard
2 teaspoons fresh lemon
  juice
1/2 teaspoon red pepper
  flakes
2/3 cup olive oil
8 ounces spinach tortellini
8 ounces egg tortellini
3 tablespoons minced onion
Basil sprigs

- COMBINE THE PEPPERONI, garlic, sun-dried tomatoes, Dijon mustard, lemon juice and pepper flakes in a food processor container. Process until finely chopped. With the motor running, add the olive oil in a thin stream.

- Prepare the spinach tortellini and egg tortellini according to package directions; drain. Toss the pasta, sauce and onion in a large bowl until the pasta is well coated. Garnish with basil. Serve at room temperature.

Orzo with Truffle Butter

MAKES **2** SERVINGS

1/2 cup orzo
1/2 cup pine nuts
1/2 cup truffle butter
2 tablespoons chopped
  parsley
Grated Parmesan cheese
  to taste

- PREPARE THE ORZO according to package directions; drain. Toast the pine nuts in a dry skillet over medium-high heat until brown, shaking the skillet to prevent burning. Combine with the orzo in a serving bowl. Add the truffle butter, parsley and Parmesan cheese and toss to mix well.

- You may serve this dish as a first course or as a luncheon entrée with a salad.

Microwave Risotto with Mushrooms

MAKES 4 SERVINGS

8 ounces sliced mushrooms
2 tablespoons butter
Salt and pepper to taste
2 cups chicken broth
3 tablespoons olive oil
1 medium onion, finely
   chopped
1 garlic clove, minced
3/4 cup arborio rice
1/2 cup grated Parmesan
   cheese

- SAUTÉ THE MUSHROOMS in the butter in a skillet until tender. Season with salt and pepper and set aside.

- Microwave the chicken broth in a 4-cup glass measuring cup on High for 3 minutes. Set aside. Microwave the olive oil in a 3-quart microwave-safe baking dish on High for 2 minutes.

- Stir in the onion and garlic. Cook on High for 3 minutes. Stir in the rice. Cook on High for 4 minutes. Stir in the hot chicken broth. Cook on High for 8 to 12 minutes or until the liquid is almost absorbed, but a sauce consistency remains.

- Cover and let stand for 5 minutes or until most of the liquid is absorbed and the rice is creamy. Drain the mushrooms and stir into the rice. Stir in the Parmesan cheese.

Green Risotto

5 cups chicken broth
1 medium onion, finely
  chopped
$1/2$ cup olive oil
$1^1/_2$ cups arborio rice
$3/_4$ cup white wine
10 fresh spinach leaves
Grated Parmesan cheese

- BRING THE CHICKEN broth to a simmer in a saucepan over medium heat. Sauté the onion in the olive oil in a heavy 3-quart saucepan until tender. Stir in the rice and cook for 1 minute. Add the white wine to the rice and cook until it is absorbed.

- Add about 1 cup of the warm chicken broth to the rice and cook until the broth is mostly absorbed, stirring constantly. Add $1/2$ cup more of the broth and cook until it is mostly absorbed, stirring constantly. Repeat this process for 20 minutes or until the rice is cooked through but al dente and the mixture is creamy.

- Wash the spinach leaves. Place the wet leaves in a blender container and purée, adding additional water if necessary. Stir the purée into the rice. Sprinkle with Parmesan cheese. Serve immediately.

- NOTE: You may not use all the broth, or you may need more. Judge by the texture of the rice, not by the amount of cooking time or liquid used.

Pesto Risotto

MAKES **4** SERVINGS

4 cups chicken broth
1/2 cup chopped onion
1 1/2 tablespoons olive oil
1 cup arborio rice
1/4 cup prepared pesto or
   Basic Pesto (at right)
3/4 cup freshly grated
   Parmesan cheese
Freshly ground pepper
   to taste

- BRING THE CHICKEN broth to a simmer in a saucepan over medium heat. Sauté the onion in the olive oil in a heavy 3-quart saucepan over medium heat until tender. Add the rice to the onion and cook for 3 minutes longer, stirring constantly.

- Add 1 cup of the warm chicken broth to the rice and cook until the broth is mostly absorbed, stirring constantly. Add another 1/2 cup of the broth and cook until it is almost absorbed. Repeat until almost all of the broth has been added.

- Stir in the pesto. Add the remaining broth in 1/4-cup amounts, cooking until the rice is al dente and the mixture is creamy. Stir in the Parmesan cheese and pepper. Serve immediately.

For **Basic Pesto,** combine 3 garlic cloves, 4 cups basil leaves, and 1 1/2 cups shredded good-quality Parmesan cheese in a food processor container. Process until finely chopped. With the motor running, add 3/4 cup olive oil in a fine stream. Add salt and pepper to taste. May store the pesto in an airtight container in the refrigerator for 3 to 4 months. Makes about 3 cups.

157

Vegetables and Side Dishes

Swan Coach House Asparagus with Orange Basil Hollandaise

MAKES 4 SERVINGS

Orange Basil Hollandaise

3 egg yolks, beaten
2 tablespoons orange juice
$1/2$ teaspoon basil
$1/4$ teaspoon salt
$1/4$ teaspoon pepper
$1/2$ cup (1 stick) unsalted
butter, cut into thirds, at
room temperature
2 tablespoons orange juice
$1^1/2$ teaspoons grated
orange zest

Asparagus

1 pound medium asparagus
spears

- FOR THE HOLLANDAISE, combine the egg yolks, 2 tablespoons orange juice, basil, salt, pepper and 1 piece of the butter in the top of a double boiler. Place over boiling water. Cook until the butter melts and the sauce begins to thicken, stirring rapidly with a wire whisk.

- Add the remaining butter 1 piece at a time, stirring constantly. Cook for 1 to 2 minutes longer or until the sauce thickens, stirring constantly. Remove from heat immediately and add the remaining 2 tablespoons orange juice and zest.

- If sauce is too thick or curdles, immediately beat in 1 to 2 tablespoons cold water.

- For the asparagus, snap off and discard tough ends of asparagus. Peel the asparagus if desired. Bring a small amount of water to a boil in a 10-inch skillet. Add the asparagus. Cook, covered, over medium heat for 5 minutes or until tender; drain. Serve the asparagus with the hollandaise.

Blender Hollandaise

MAKES ¾ CUP

3 egg yolks
2 tablespoons lemon juice
¼ teaspoon salt
Pinch of red pepper
½ cup (1 stick) butter,
  melted

- COMBINE THE EGG yolks, lemon juice, salt and red pepper in a blender container. Process at low speed, pouring the butter into the blender in a slow steady stream. Heat in the top of a double boiler set over simmering water.

- NOTE: May store, covered, in the refrigerator after blending and heat over simmering water when ready to use.

Mean Baked Beans

MAKES 12 SERVINGS

2 (18-ounce) cans pork and
  beans
1 (21-ounce) can apple pie
  filling
1 pound hot bulk pork
  sausage, browned and
  drained
2 tablespoons molasses
¼ cup steak sauce
¼ cup barbecue sauce

- COMBINE THE PORK and beans, apple pie filling, sausage, molasses, steak sauce and barbecue sauce in a large bowl and mix well. Spoon into a baking dish. Bake at 350 degrees for 1½ hours.

Creamy Carrots with Cheese

3/4 cup chicken consommé
1/2 teaspoon salt
1/2 teaspoon sugar
*2 pounds carrots, peeled
  and sliced*
1/4 cup (1/2 stick) butter
*6 ounces Velveeta cheese,
  cut into cubes*
2 tablespoons sour cream
*1 leek, white part only, thinly
  sliced*
*2 tablespoons chopped
  parsley*

- BRING THE CONSOMMÉ, salt and sugar to a boil in a large saucepan. Add the carrots and cook, covered, for 8 to 10 minutes or until tender; drain. Add the butter.

- Mix the cheese, sour cream and leek in a bowl. Add to the carrots but do not stir. Simmer, covered, over low heat for 2 to 3 minutes or until the cheese is melted. Sprinkle with the parsley to serve.

Carrot Pudding

3 egg yolks

$1/2$ cup sugar

$3/4$ cup ($1^1/2$ sticks) unsalted butter

$3/4$ cup flour

2 pounds carrots, finely chopped, cooked

$1/2$ cup shredded Cheddar cheese

$1^1/2$ teaspoons baking powder

4 egg whites

2 cups walnut pieces

2 tablespoons unsalted butter

$1/4$ cup sugar

- BEAT THE EGG yolks and $1/2$ cup sugar in a mixing bowl until light and fluffy. Add the $3/4$ cup butter and flour alternately until all are incorporated. Add the carrots and cheese and mix lightly. Fold in the baking powder.

- Beat the egg whites in a mixing bowl until soft peaks form. Stir a small amount of the egg whites into the carrot batter to lighten it. Fold in the remaining whites.

- Pour the mixture into a greased 3-quart soufflé dish or a 9x13-inch baking pan. Bake at 300 degrees for 30 minutes or until a wooden pick inserted in the center comes out clean.

- Sauté the walnuts in the 2 tablespoons butter in a skillet for about 1 minute. Sprinkle with the $1/4$ cup sugar. Spoon the walnuts over the pudding just before serving.

Stewed Corn

MAKES **6** SERVINGS

4 ears fresh corn
1 onion, thinly sliced
2 tablespoons unsalted
   butter
1 tablespoon vegetable oil
1 tomato, seeded and
   chopped
$1/2$ cup heavy cream
$1/4$ cup water
Salt and pepper to taste
Fried Okra (page 165)

- CUT THE CORN from the cobs and scrape the remaining pulp from the cobs. This should equal about 3 cups of corn.

- Cook the onion in the butter and oil in a large skillet over medium heat until golden brown, stirring occasionally.

- Add the corn, tomato, cream and water and mix well. Cook, covered, over medium-low heat for 20 minutes. Add salt and pepper and keep warm.

- Serve the stewed corn topped with the Fried Okra.

Fried Okra

MAKES **6** SERVINGS

4 ounces okra
Cornmeal
Salt and pepper to taste
Vegetable oil

- CUT THE OKRA into 1/4-inch slices. Combine the cornmeal, salt and pepper in a bowl and mix well. Toss the okra with the cornmeal mixture. Pour the okra into a sieve and shake to remove excess cornmeal.

- Heat 1/2 inch oil in a deep skillet until hot but not smoking (about 365 degrees). Fry the okra in batches for 1 to 2 minutes or until golden brown. Drain on paper towels.

For **Super-Quick Corn,** microwave corn in the husk for 2 minutes per ear on High. Wear rubber gloves when shucking and cleaning. Corn is hot and ready to serve.

Herb-Scented Corn

MAKES **4** SERVINGS

3 cups fresh or thawed
   frozen corn
2/3 cup heavy cream
1 teaspoon minced fresh
   thyme
Salt and pepper to taste
1/4 cup fresh bread crumbs

- COMBINE THE CORN, cream, thyme, salt and pepper in a bowl and mix well. Spoon into a greased 1- to 2-quart baking dish. Sprinkle with the bread crumbs.

- Bake at 350 degrees for 25 minutes or until crusty around the edges. Broil about 4 inches from the heat source for 2 minutes or until the bread crumbs are toasted.

Cauliflower Panache

2 quarts water
2 tablespoons salt
1 large cauliflower, broken
    into florets
3 tablespoons grated
    Parmesan cheese
1 large bunch broccoli,
    stalks peeled
2 tablespoons butter
1/4 cup sour cream
Salt and pepper to taste
1/3 cup bread crumbs

- BRING THE WATER and 2 tablespoons salt to a boil in a large saucepan over high heat. Add the cauliflower. Cook, covered, for 5 minutes or until tender. Remove the cauliflower, reserving the water. Place the cauliflower in a 1 1/2-quart baking dish. Sprinkle with the Parmesan cheese.

- Bring the reserved water to a boil. Add the broccoli, standing it up. Cover with cheesecloth and cook for 8 minutes or until tender but still bright green. (You may microwave the broccoli instead, as this also helps retain the color.)

- Chop the broccoli coarsely and place in a food processor or blender container with the butter and sour cream. Add salt and pepper to taste. Process to a purée.

- Spoon the purée over the cauliflower, completely covering it. Sprinkle with the bread crumbs. Bake at 350 degrees for 20 minutes.

Cranberry Apple Casserole

3 cups chopped unpeeled
   apples
2 cups whole fresh
   cranberries
$1/2$ cup sugar
$1/3$ cup packed brown sugar
$1/2$ cup (1 stick) butter
$1/4$ cup packed brown sugar
1 cup rolled oats
$1/3$ cup flour
$1/3$ cup chopped pecans

- COMBINE THE APPLES and cranberries in a bowl and mix well. Spoon into a buttered $1^{1}/2$-quart baking dish. Combine the sugar and $1/3$ cup brown sugar in a small bowl and mix well. Sprinkle over the top.

- Melt the butter in a medium saucepan or microwave-safe bowl. Add the $1/4$ cup brown sugar, oats, flour and pecans to the bowl and mix well. Spoon over the cranberries. Bake at 350 degrees for 45 minutes.

Braised Red Cabbage

MAKES 6 TO 8 SERVINGS

1 small head red cabbage,
    sliced
1/4 cup sugar
1 tablespoon salt
1 cup red wine vinegar
1/4 cup (1/2 stick) butter or
    margarine
1 onion, sliced
1 apple, peeled, cored and
    diced
1/2 cup red currant jelly
1/4 cup hot water
1/8 teaspoon cloves
1/4 teaspoon cinnamon

- COMBINE THE CABBAGE, sugar, salt and vinegar in a bowl and let stand for 15 minutes.

- Melt the butter in a 5-quart saucepan over medium heat. Add the onion and cook for 5 minutes or until transparent. Add the apple and sauté for 5 minutes longer. Add the cabbage mixture to the saucepan. Bring to a boil and reduce heat to low.

- Combine the jelly, water, cloves and cinnamon in a bowl and mix well. Add to the saucepan. Simmer, covered, for 1 hour or until tender. Serve immediately.

Gingery Cabbage and Carrots

MAKES 4 SERVINGS

4 medium carrots
   (about 8 ounces)
16 ounces red cabbage
Salt to taste
2 tablespoons butter
1 teaspoon minced, peeled
   fresh ginger
2 teaspoons soy sauce
1/2 teaspoon sugar

- CUT THE CARROTS and cabbage into julienne strips. Cook the carrots in boiling salted water in a saucepan for 2 minutes or until just tender-crisp. Remove the carrots from the water with a slotted spoon and place in a bowl. Add the cabbage to the water and boil for 1 minute or until just tender-crisp; drain.

- Melt the butter in a large skillet over medium-high heat. Add the ginger and cook for 30 seconds, stirring constantly. Add the carrots, cabbage, soy sauce and sugar. Cook for 2 minutes, stirring constantly.

Creole Eggplant and Tomato Casserole

1 large eggplant, peeled
  and chopped
1 cup chopped celery
1 green bell pepper,
  chopped
2 (15-ounce) cans tomatoes
2 onions, chopped
1 teaspoon salt
Pepper to taste
1 teaspoon MSG
1 teaspoon Worcestershire
  sauce
1 teaspoon sugar
Dash of Tabasco sauce
6 tablespoons (¾ stick)
  butter
3 slices bread, torn into
  pieces
Bread crumbs
Butter

- RINSE AND DRAIN the eggplant. Combine the eggplant, celery and bell pepper in a Dutch oven. Add the tomatoes, onions, salt, pepper, MSG, Worcestershire sauce, sugar, Tabasco sauce, 6 tablespoons butter and bread and mix well. Bring to a boil.

- Cook over medium heat until most of the liquid is evaporated. Pour the mixture into a baking dish. Sprinkle with bread crumbs and dot with butter. Bake at 350 degrees for 45 minutes.

Green Beans with Red Onion and Mint

MAKES **6** SERVINGS

2 pounds green beans, trimmed
1 tablespoon white wine vinegar
1 teaspoon Dijon mustard
Salt and pepper to taste
$1/4$ cup olive oil
3 tablespoons minced fresh mint
$1/2$ cup minced red onion

- COOK THE GREEN beans in boiling water in a large saucepan for 2 to 4 minutes or until tender-crisp; drain. Cover with cold water and drain again. Chill, covered, for 3 to 12 hours.

- Combine the vinegar, mustard, salt and pepper in a large bowl and mix well. Pour in the oil, whisking until well blended. Add the green beans, mint and onion. Toss until well combined.

For **Green Beans with Pine Nuts,** cook 1 pound trimmed green beans in a covered saucepan in 1 inch of water for 4 to 8 minutes or until tender-crisp. Melt 2 tablespoons butter in a large skillet over medium heat. Add 2 tablespoons pine nuts and cook until the pine nuts are golden brown, stirring frequently. Add the green beans to the skillet. Stir to coat with the butter. Season with salt and pepper to taste. Makes 4 servings.

Red Peppers Stuffed with Tomato and Mozzarella

MAKES 4 SERVINGS

3 red bell peppers
1 1/2 teaspoons extra-virgin
  olive oil
1 garlic clove, minced
1 1/2 tablespoons balsamic
  vinegar
Salt and pepper to taste
12 ounces cherry tomatoes,
  stemmed and halved
1 cup cubed mozzarella
  cheese
1/2 cup loosely packed fresh
  basil leaves, cut into strips

- CUT THE BELL peppers into halves lengthwise. Remove the seeds and ribs. Cut a thin slice from the rounded side of each pepper half so it will sit securely in a baking dish.

- Combine the olive oil, garlic, vinegar, salt and pepper in a bowl, whisking until blended. Add the tomatoes, cheese and basil and mix well. Fill each pepper with the tomato mixture. Place the filled peppers in a baking dish. Bake at 375 degrees for 40 minutes or until the peppers are tender.

Potato Gratin with Boursin

MAKES 8 SERVINGS

2 cups heavy cream
1 (5-ounce) package boursin
  cheese with herbs
5 medium baking potatoes,
  thinly sliced
Salt and pepper to taste
1¹/₂ tablespoons chopped
  fresh parsley

- COMBINE THE HEAVY cream and cheese in a large saucepan. Cook over medium heat until the cheese is melted and the mixture is well blended, stirring constantly.

- Arrange half of the unpeeled potato slices in slightly overlapping rows in a greased 9x13-inch baking dish. Sprinkle generously with salt and pepper. Pour half of the cheese mixture over the potatoes. Arrange the remaining potato slices over the cheese mixture. Sprinkle generously with salt and pepper. Top with remaining cheese mixture.

- Bake at 400 degrees for 1 hour or until the top is golden brown and the potatoes are tender. Sprinkle the parsley over the top.

- NOTE: You may serve immediately or store, covered, in the refrigerator for 1 day to improve the flavor.

Scalloped Potatoes with Truffle Crema

2 medium baking potatoes,
   thinly sliced
1 small onion, chopped
1 tablespoon vegetable oil
40 grams (¹/₂ jar) white or
   black truffle crema
¹/₄ cup heavy cream
¹/₄ cup chicken stock
¹/₄ to ¹/₂ cup shredded
   Gruyère or smoked
   Gouda cheese

- BOIL THE POTATO slices in enough water to cover in a saucepan for 3 to 4 minutes or until tender-crisp; drain.

- Sauté the onion in the oil in a skillet until tender. Arrange the potatoes and onion in a small greased baking dish.

- Combine the truffle crema, heavy cream and chicken stock in a small bowl and mix well. Pour over the potatoes and onion. Sprinkle the cheese over the top.

- Bake at 350 degrees for 45 minutes or until the cheese is brown.

- NOTE: This dish is a wonderful accompaniment to roasted or grilled meat, fish or poultry.

Sweet Potato Soufflé

Soufflé

3 cups mashed cooked
   sweet potatoes
3/4 cup sugar
1/2 teaspoon salt
2 eggs, lightly beaten
3 tablespoons butter, melted
1/2 cup milk
1 teaspoon vanilla extract

Pecan Topping

3 tablespoons butter, melted
1 cup packed brown sugar
1/3 cup flour
1 cup chopped pecans

- FOR THE SOUFFLÉ, combine the sweet potatoes, sugar, salt, eggs, butter, milk and vanilla in a bowl and mix well. Spoon into a greased 1-quart baking dish.

- For the topping, combine the butter, brown sugar, flour and pecans in a bowl and mix until crumbly. Sprinkle over the sweet potato mixture.

- Bake, covered, at 350 degrees for 25 minutes. Uncover and bake for 10 minutes or until the top is brown and firm to the touch.

Martini Sauerkraut

MAKES 6 TO 8 SERVINGS

2 pounds prepared
  sauerkraut
5 ounces bacon
1 cup thinly sliced onions
1 cup gin
$1/2$ cup vermouth
1 (10-ounce) can chicken
  broth
Salt and pepper to taste

- RINSE THE SAUERKRAUT and drain well, squeezing out excess moisture. Chop the bacon. Cook the bacon with the onions in a skillet over low heat for 10 minutes, stirring frequently; do not allow the onion or bacon to brown.

- Add the sauerkraut, gin and vermouth to the skillet and mix well. Spoon the sauerkraut mixture into a baking dish. Pour enough chicken broth over the sauerkraut mixture to cover. Season with salt and pepper. Bake, covered, at 350 degrees for 3 to 4 hours.

Tomatoes Rockefeller

6 large tomatoes, or
   9 medium tomatoes
Garlic salt to taste
2 (10-ounce) packages
   frozen chopped spinach,
   cooked and drained
1½ teaspoons (or more)
   minced onion
1 teaspoon MSG
½ cup grated Parmesan
   cheese
½ teaspoon pepper
¼ teaspoon Tabasco sauce
2 eggs, lightly beaten
½ cup (1 stick) butter,
   melted
Salt to taste

- CUT A THIN slice from the top of each tomato and scoop out the pulp, leaving a thick shell. Sprinkle the inside with garlic salt.

- Combine the spinach, onion, MSG, cheese, pepper, Tabasco sauce, eggs, butter and salt in a bowl and mix well. Fill each tomato with the spinach mixture. Arrange filled tomatoes in a baking dish. Bake at 350 degrees for 30 minutes.

Stuffed Zucchini Boats

MAKES 4 TO 6 SERVINGS

Zucchini

8 to 10 young slender
  zucchini, 6 to 8 inches
  long
Salt to taste

White Sauce

2 tablespoons butter
1 1/2 tablespoons flour
1 cup milk
Salt to taste
Pinch of nutmeg

Prosciutto Stuffing

2 tablespoons butter
1 tablespoon vegetable oil
1 tablespoon finely
  chopped onion
4 ounces chopped prosciutto
1 egg, lightly beaten
1/4 cup grated Parmesan
  cheese

Assembly

Fine dry bread crumbs
Butter

- FOR THE ZUCCHINI, trim the ends of the zucchini and cut into halves lengthwise. Scoop out the seeds and pulp, leaving a 1/4- to 1/2-inch-thick shell; reserve half of the pulp. Chop the reserved pulp and set aside for the stuffing. Cook the zucchini shells in boiling salted water in a saucepan for 3 to 5 minutes or until tender-crisp; drain.

- For the sauce, melt the butter in a medium saucepan over medium-low heat. Add the flour and mix well. Whisk in the milk. Cook until thickened, stirring constantly. Season with salt and nutmeg. Set aside.

- For the stuffing, heat the butter and oil in a skillet. Sauté the onion, prosciutto and reserved zucchini pulp in the skillet over medium-high heat until tender. Remove from the skillet with a slotted spoon. Add the vegetables to the white sauce in the saucepan and mix well. Add the egg and cheese and mix well.

- To assemble, spoon the stuffing into the zucchini shells. Sprinkle with bread crumbs. Dot with butter. Arrange the zucchini boats in a greased rectangular baking dish. Bake at 400 degrees for 20 minutes.

- NOTE: This dish should not be made more than a few hours in advance.

Garlicky Oven-Roasted Vegetables

MAKES 8 SERVINGS

2¹/₂ pounds rutabagas
2 pounds onions
1 pound sweet potatoes
6 tablespoons olive oil
30 garlic cloves
14 to 16 sage leaves,
    crumbled or torn
7 sprigs of fresh rosemary,
    torn
Salt and pepper to taste

- HEAT 2 LARGE HEAVY roasting pans in a 450-degree oven for 15 minutes.

- Peel the rutabagas, onions and sweet potatoes and cut into 1-inch chunks.

- Add 1 tablespoon of olive oil to each pan. Add half of the vegetables, garlic, sage and rosemary to each pan. Drizzle the vegetables in each pan with 2 tablespoons olive oil. Season with salt and pepper to taste. Roast the vegetables for 1¹/₄ hours or until tender when pierced with a fork, stirring occasionally.

- NOTE: You may add turnips or carrots to the vegetable mixture, or substitute one or both for the rutabagas or sweet potatoes.

Winter Vegetable Crowns

MAKES 8 SERVINGS

1 head cauliflower
1 head broccoflower
1 bunch broccoli
1/2 cup (1 stick) butter
2 to 3 garlic cloves, minced
Grated Parmesan cheese to
    taste
Toasted pine nuts

- CUT THE CAULIFLOWER, broccoflower and broccoli into florets. Steam the vegetables separately over boiling water or in a microwave-safe vegetable steamer until tender-crisp. Cover with cold water to stop the cooking process.

- Melt the butter in a large skillet. Add the garlic and cook for 1 minute. Add the florets and stir to coat. Cook until heated through. Spoon onto a serving platter. Top with Parmesan cheese and toasted pine nuts.

Ratatouille

2 large onions, sliced
3 green bell peppers,
  chopped
6 tablespoons vegetable oil
2 zucchini, sliced
1 small eggplant, peeled
  and chopped
1 (29-ounce) can plum
  tomatoes, drained,
  chopped
2 teaspoons salt
2 garlic cloves, crushed
3 tablespoons chopped
  parsley

- SAUTÉ THE ONIONS and bell peppers in the oil in a large skillet until the onions begin to turn golden brown. Add the zucchini, eggplant, tomatoes and salt and mix well.

- Simmer, covered, for 40 minutes or until very tender. Add the garlic and parsley and simmer for 2 minutes. Adjust seasonings.

Mushroom Cheese Pie

MAKES **6** SERVINGS

For **Pie Pastry,** combine 2 cups sifted flour and 1 teaspoon salt in a bowl and mix well. Cut in 2/3 cup shortening with two knives or a pastry cutter until the mixture resembles coarse crumbs. Add 4 to 5 tablespoons ice water and stir with a fork until the dough holds together. Refrigerate the dough for 10 minutes before working. Makes enough pastry for a 2-crust pie.

1 1/2 pounds mushrooms, sliced
1 cup thinly sliced onion
1/4 cup (1/2 stick) butter
1/3 cup flour
8 ounces cream-style cottage cheese
1/4 cup chopped parsley
1/4 cup dry sherry
1 teaspoon salt
1/8 teaspoon pepper
Pastry for a 2-crust pie (at left)

- SAUTÉ THE MUSHROOMS and onion in the butter in a large skillet until tender. Add the flour and mix well. Add the cottage cheese, parsley, sherry, salt and pepper to the skillet and mix well.

- Divide the dough in half. Roll each half into a 12-inch circle on a lightly floured board. Line a 9-inch pie dish with 1 of the circles, trimming off any excess pastry.

- Pour the mushroom mixture into the pastry-lined dish. Cut the remaining pastry into 1/2-inch strips. Arrange the strips in lattice fashion over the mushroom mixture. Crimp the edges to seal.

- Bake at 425 degrees for 20 to 25 minutes on the bottom oven rack. Cover the crust with foil and bake for 20 minutes longer. Let stand for 5 minutes before slicing.

Vidalia Onion Pie

MAKES 6 SERVINGS

1 cup crushed butter-flavor crackers

1/4 cup (1/2 stick) butter, melted

3 cups chopped Vidalia onions

2 tablespoons butter

2 eggs

3/4 cup milk

1/2 teaspoon salt

1/4 teaspoon pepper

1 cup shredded Cheddar cheese

1/8 teaspoon paprika

• COMBINE THE CRACKERS and 1/4 cup melted butter in a bowl and mix well. Press into a greased pie dish.

• Sauté the onions in the 2 tablespoons butter in a skillet until tender. Spoon the onions into the crust. Combine the eggs, milk, salt and pepper in a bowl and mix well. Pour over the onions.

• Sprinkle the cheese over the top. Dust with the paprika. Bake at 350 degrees for 30 minutes. Let stand for 5 minutes before slicing.

Spinach Pie

1/2 large purple onion,
   chopped
1 tablespoon butter
1 (10-ounce) package
   frozen chopped spinach,
   thawed
1 cup heavy cream
1 (6-ounce) can pitted black
   olives, drained, sliced
1/2 teaspoon nutmeg
2 eggs, lightly beaten
1 2/3 cups grated Parmesan
   cheese
1 unbaked (9-inch) pie shell

- SAUTÉ THE ONION in the butter in a skillet until tender. Squeeze the excess moisture from the spinach. Combine the onion, spinach, heavy cream, olives, nutmeg, eggs and cheese in a bowl and mix well. Pour into the pie shell.

- Bake at 350 degrees for 30 to 45 minutes or until set in the center. Let cool before slicing.

Cool Rice Pilaf

MAKES 8 SERVINGS

1 (4- to 6-ounce) package
   yellow or spicy rice mix
2 (6-ounce) jars marinated
   artichoke hearts
1/3 cup mayonnaise
3/4 teaspoon curry powder
4 scallions, sliced
1/2 green bell pepper,
   chopped
12 stuffed green olives,
   chopped

- COOK THE RICE according to package directions. Cool completely. Drain the artichoke hearts, reserving the liquid.

- Combine the mayonnaise, curry powder and reserved artichoke liquid in a large bowl and mix well. Add the rice, artichoke hearts, scallions, bell pepper and olives to the bowl and mix well.

- NOTE: This dish is delicious cold, or you may mix the ingredients together while the rice is still warm for a hot side dish.

For **Restaurant Rice,** combine 2 cups water, 1 cup basmati rice, 1 teaspoon salt and 1 tablespoon butter in a baking dish and mix well. Bake, covered, at 350 degrees for 1 hour; do not stir. Makes 2 or 3 servings.

185

Almond Raisin Rice

MAKES **6** SERVINGS

2¼ cups water
2 cups apple juice
2 cups converted rice
¾ cup raisins
1 tablespoon sugar
2 teaspoons salt
2 tablespoons butter
½ cup slivered almonds

- COMBINE THE WATER and apple juice in a medium saucepan. Bring to a boil over medium-high heat. Add the rice, raisins, sugar and salt and mix well. Cook, covered, over low heat for 25 minutes or until all the liquid is absorbed.

- Heat the butter in a skillet over medium-high heat and add the almonds. Cook until the almonds are golden brown and toasted. Fold into the cooked rice. Serve with your favorite curried dishes.

Nutted Wild Rice

MAKES 6 TO 8 SERVINGS

1 cup golden raisins
1/2 cup dry sherry
2 cups chicken stock or
   broth
1 cup wild rice
2 tablespoons unsalted
   butter
2²/3 cups chicken stock or
   broth
1 cup brown rice
2 tablespoons unsalted
   butter
1 cup slivered almonds
2 tablespoons unsalted
   butter
1/2 cup chopped fresh
   parsley
Salt and pepper to taste

- HEAT THE RAISINS and sherry in a saucepan over medium heat for 5 minutes; set aside.

- Bring the 2 cups chicken stock to a boil in the top of a double boiler. Add the wild rice and 2 tablespoons butter. Cook, covered, over simmering water for 1 hour.

- Bring the 2²/3 cups chicken stock to a boil in a saucepan. Add the brown rice and 2 tablespoons butter. Cook, covered, over low heat for 50 minutes or until the rice is tender.

- Sauté the almonds in the 2 tablespoons butter in a skillet until lightly toasted. Combine the raisins with sherry, wild rice, brown rice, almonds, parsley, salt and pepper in a serving bowl and mix well.

Louisiana Cheese Grits

MAKES 6 TO 8 SERVINGS

1 1/2 cups grits (not instant)
6 cups water
1/2 cup (1 stick) butter,
  softened
8 ounces Velveeta cheese,
  cut into chunks
8 ounces sharp Cheddar
  cheese, shredded
1/2 cup sautéed chopped
  onion
3 tablespoons chopped
  pimentos
1 tablespoon seasoned salt
3 eggs

- COOK THE GRITS in the water according to package directions, omitting the salt. Stir in the butter, Velveeta cheese, Cheddar cheese, onion, pimentos and salt and mix well. Let cool slightly. Beat the eggs in a bowl. Stir into the grits mixture and mix well. Spoon the mixture into a greased baking dish.

- Bake at 350 degrees for 1 hour. Let stand for 10 minutes or more before serving. Serve with meats, fish or game as a side dish or with eggs for brunch.

Magic Sweet Pickles

MAKES 4 QUARTS OR 8 PINTS

4 (46-ounce) jars
 (or 1-gallon jar) kosher
 dill pickles
5 pounds sugar
4 cinnamon sticks, broken
 into halves
4 garlic cloves, cut into
 halves
2 tablespoons mustard seeds
2 tablespoons whole
 peppercorns

- DRAIN THE PICKLES and discard the liquid. Cut the pickles into 1/4-inch slices

- Combine the sugar, cinnamon sticks, garlic, mustard seeds and peppercorns in a large bowl and mix well. Alternate layers of the pickle slices and sugar mixture in clean sterile jars. Screw on sterile lids. Turn the jars upside down. Refrigerate for 6 days before using.

For **Quick Cranberry Relish,** combine 1 quart cranberries, 2 coarsely chopped Granny Smith apples, 1 coarsely chopped orange, 1 coarsely chopped lemon and 1 1/2 cups sugar in a food processor container. Process until finely ground. Spoon into a serving bowl. Refrigerate, covered, until ready to use. Makes about 5 cups.

Chocolate Sheet Cake

MAKES 30 TO 40 SERVINGS

5 tablespoons baking cocoa
1 cup water
1 cup (2 sticks) butter
2 cups flour
2 cups sugar
1/2 teaspoon salt
1 teaspoon vanilla extract
2 eggs, beaten
1 teaspoon baking soda
1/2 cup buttermilk
Fudge Nut Icing (below)

- COMBINE THE BAKING cocoa, water and butter in a saucepan. Heat over medium heat until the butter melts, stirring occasionally. Combine the flour, sugar and salt in a large bowl and mix well. Beat in the butter mixture. Beat in the vanilla and eggs.

- Dissolve the baking soda in the buttermilk and add to the chocolate mixture; mix well. Spoon the mixture into a greased 10x15- or 12x16-inch baking pan. Bake at 350 degrees for 20 minutes. Remove from the oven. Pour Fudge Nut Icing over the hot cake. Cool before cutting into squares.

Fudge Nut Icing

MAKES ABOUT 5 CUPS

1/2 cup (1 stick) butter
6 tablespoons milk
6 tablespoons (rounded) baking cocoa
1 pound confectioners' sugar
2/3 cup chopped walnuts

- COMBINE THE BUTTER, milk and baking cocoa in a medium saucepan over low heat, stirring occasionally. Stir in the confectioners' sugar and walnuts.

Grand Marnier Chocolate Cake

14 ounces semisweet
  chocolate
3/4 cup (1 1/2 sticks) plus
  2 tablespoons unsalted
  butter
10 egg yolks
1 cup sugar
1 tablespoon vanilla extract
1 tablespoon Grand Marnier
1 teaspoon lemon juice
10 egg whites
1/2 cup sugar
Confectioners' sugar
2 cups whipping cream,
  whipped

- MELT THE CHOCOLATE and butter in the top of a double boiler over simmering water. Beat the egg yolks with 1 cup sugar in a bowl until well blended. Stir in the vanilla, Grand Marnier and lemon juice. Stir in the chocolate mixture.

- Beat the egg whites in a mixing bowl until soft peaks form. Beat in the 1/2 cup sugar until stiff peaks form. Stir 1 cup of the egg white mixture into the chocolate mixture. Fold in the remaining egg white mixture. Spoon the batter into a greased and floured 12-inch springform pan.

- Bake at 250 degrees for 2 1/2 hours. Cool in the pan for 10 minutes. Remove the side of the pan and cool completely. Sprinkle with confectioners' sugar. Serve with the whipped cream.

Chocolate Roulage

For **Vanilla Whipped Cream,** beat 2 cups whipping cream in a chilled mixing bowl, adding 1/4 cup sugar gradually. Beat in 1 teaspoon vanilla extract. Refrigerate the whipped cream until ready to use.

6 ounces semisweet chocolate
3 tablespoons water
6 large egg yolks
1 cup sugar
6 large egg whites
2 tablespoons butter or margarine, melted
1/4 cup (about) baking cocoa
Vanilla Whipped Cream (at left)

- MELT THE CHOCOLATE in the water in a small saucepan over low heat.

- Beat the egg yolks in a large mixing bowl for 2 1/2 minutes, adding the sugar gradually. Beat the egg whites in a separate mixing bowl until stiff peaks form. Stir the chocolate mixture into the egg yolk mixture. Fold in the egg whites.

- Brush 1 tablespoon of the butter over the bottom of a 9x12-inch or a 10x15-inch cake pan. Cut a sheet of waxed paper to fit the width of the pan and extend a few inches over the ends. Brush the remaining 1 tablespoon butter over the waxed paper. Spread the batter in the prepared pan. Bake at 350 degrees for 30 minutes.

- Remove cake from oven. Place 2 or 3 damp paper towels on top of the cake. Let cake cool on a wire rack for at least 30 minutes.

- Remove the paper towels from the cake. Sift the baking cocoa over the cake. Place a sheet of waxed paper over the cake and place a baking sheet over the waxed paper. Invert the cake. Peel the waxed paper from the inverted cake. Spread Vanilla Whipped Cream over the cake. Roll up about 4 inches of the cake from the short end; press in place. Roll the cake to enclose whipped cream, twisting the ends of the waxed paper to hold it in place. Refrigerate the cake for 1 hour or longer before serving. Cut into 1-inch slices to serve.

Cola Cake

2 cups flour
2 cups sugar
3 tablespoons baking cocoa
1 teaspoon baking soda
1/2 teaspoon salt
1/2 cup vegetable oil
1/2 cup (1 stick) butter
1 cup cola
1/2 cup buttermilk
2 eggs, lightly beaten
2 cups miniature
    marshmallows
1 teaspoon vanilla extract
Chocolate Cola Icing
    (below)

- COMBINE THE FLOUR, sugar, baking cocoa, baking soda and salt in a bowl and mix well. Combine the oil, butter and cola in a large saucepan and mix well. Bring to a boil over medium-high heat.

- Add the flour mixture to the saucepan and mix well. Add the buttermilk, eggs, marshmallows and vanilla to the saucepan and mix well; the batter will be thin. Spoon into a greased 9-inch square pan or small rectangular pan. Bake at 350 degrees for 45 minutes. Pour Chocolate Cola Icing over the hot cake.

Chocolate Cola Icing

MAKES ABOUT **3** CUPS

1/2 cup (1 stick) butter
3 tablespoons baking cocoa
6 tablespoons cola
1 pound confectioners'
    sugar
1 teaspoon vanilla extract
1 cup chopped nuts
    (optional)

- COMBINE THE BUTTER, baking cocoa and cola in a small saucepan. Bring to a boil over medium-high heat. Pour over the confectioners' sugar in a large bowl and mix well. Stir in the vanilla and nuts.

Old-Fashioned Fig Cake

MAKES **12** TO **16** SERVINGS

2 cups flour
1 teaspoon salt
1 teaspoon baking soda
1 1/2 cups sugar
1 cup vegetable oil
3 eggs
1 cup buttermilk
1 cup fig preserves
1 cup chopped pecans
1 teaspoon cinnamon
1 teaspoon nutmeg
1 teaspoon vanilla extract
Buttermilk Glaze (below)

- SIFT THE FLOUR, salt, baking soda and sugar into a bowl and mix well. Add the oil and mix well. Beat in the eggs 1 at a time. Add the buttermilk and preserves. Stir in the pecans, cinnamon, nutmeg and vanilla.

- Spoon the batter into a greased and floured bundt pan. Bake at 325 degrees for 1 1/2 hours. Cool in pan for 10 minutes. Invert onto a platter. Poke holes in the cake with a wooden pick. Brush or drizzle warm Buttermilk Glaze over the cake.

Buttermilk Glaze

MAKES ABOUT **1** CUP

1/2 cup sugar
1/4 cup (1/2 stick) butter
2 teaspoons light corn syrup
1/2 teaspoon vanilla extract
1/8 teaspoon baking soda
1/4 cup buttermilk

- COMBINE THE SUGAR, butter, corn syrup, vanilla, baking soda and buttermilk in a saucepan. Bring to a boil over medium-high heat. Boil for 3 minutes, stirring frequently.

Lemon Queens with Lemon Frosting

1¹/₂ cups sifted cake flour
¹/₄ teaspoon salt
¹/₄ teaspoon baking soda
¹/₂ cup (1 stick) butter, softened
1 cup sugar
4 egg yolks, beaten
1 teaspoon (scant) lemon juice
Grated zest of 1 lemon
4 egg whites
Lemon Frosting (below)

- SIFT THE FLOUR, salt and baking soda into a medium bowl. Cream the butter and sugar in a large mixing bowl until fluffy. Add the egg yolks, lemon juice and lemon zest. Add the flour mixture gradually, mixing well after each addition.

- Beat the egg whites in a mixing bowl until stiff peaks form. Fold into the batter. Spoon into greased muffin cups. Bake at 350 degrees for 20 minutes. Cool in pan for 10 minutes. Remove to a wire rack to cool completely. Frost the tops with Lemon Frosting.

Lemon Frosting

MAKES ABOUT **1** CUP

3 tablespoons butter, softened
1¹/₂ cups confectioners' sugar
2 teaspoons lemon juice
Dash of salt
Grated zest of ¹/₄ lemon

- CREAM THE BUTTER and confectioners' sugar in a mixing bowl until light and fluffy. Add the lemon juice gradually, beating constantly. Stir in the salt and lemon zest.

Piña Colada Cake

MAKES 18 SERVINGS

1 (18-ounce) package
   yellow cake mix
1 (14-ounce) can sweetened
   condensed milk
1 (15-ounce) can cream of
   coconut
1 (14-ounce) bag shredded
   sweetened coconut
1 (8-ounce) can crushed
   pineapple
8 ounces whipped topping

- PREPARE AND BAKE the cake mix according to package directions for a 9x13-inch cake pan. Remove from the oven and poke holes in the top of the cake with the handle of a wooden spoon.

- Combine the sweetened condensed milk, cream of coconut and half of the shredded coconut in a bowl and mix well. Pour over the hot cake. Let stand until the cake absorbs the liquid. Spread the undrained pineapple over the cake. Cool completely.

- Combine the remaining coconut with the whipped topping in a bowl and mix well. Spread over the top of the cake. Refrigerate, covered, for 24 hours before serving.

White Chocolate Ginger Cheesecake

MAKES 12 TO 16 SERVINGS

Gingersnap Crust (at right)
1 pound good-quality white
  chocolate, finely chopped
32 ounces cream cheese,
  softened
1/4 cup sugar
4 large eggs, at room
  temperature
1 large egg yolk, at room
  temperature
1 tablespoon vanilla extract
1 teaspoon ground ginger
2/3 cup minced crystallized
  ginger

- BUTTER A 9-INCH springform pan with a 2³/₄-inch side. Wrap 2 layers of foil around the outside of the pan to prevent leakage. Press the Gingersnap Crust over the bottom and up the side of the prepared pan. Refrigerate until ready to use.

- Heat the white chocolate in the top of a double boiler set over simmering water until it melts, stirring occasionally. Cool to lukewarm.

- Beat the cream cheese and sugar in a large mixing bowl for 3 minutes or until fluffy. Add the eggs and the egg yolk 1 at a time, beating just until mixed after each addition. Beat in the vanilla and ground ginger. Beat in the white chocolate gradually. Stir in the crystallized ginger.

- Spoon the filling into the prepared crust. Place the springform pan in a large roasting or other large flat pan. Add enough water to the roasting pan to reach halfway up the side of the springform pan.

- Bake in the center of a 300-degree oven for 1¹/₂ hours or until cheesecake puffs and the edges crack slightly. Cool on a wire rack. Run a small knife between the cake and the side of the pan to loosen. Cool completely. Remove foil from the pan. Refrigerate cake overnight. Remove side of the pan before slicing.

For **Gingersnap Crust**, process 13 ounces gingersnap cookies (about 50 cookies), 2 tablespoons sugar and 1 teaspoon ground ginger in a food processor until fine crumbs form. Add 6¹/₂ tablespoons cooled melted unsalted butter and process until the mixture forms clumps.

201

Yellow Cake with Butterscotch Icing

MAKES **10** TO **12** SERVINGS

For **Simple Butterscotch Icing,** combine 1 cup (2 sticks) butter, 2 cups packed light brown sugar and 1/2 cup evaporated milk in a large saucepan. Bring to a boil over medium-high heat, stirring constantly. Boil for 1 minute. Remove from the heat and add one (1-pound) package confectioners' sugar and a pinch of salt. Beat lightly with a spoon. Spread warm icing over favorite cake. Makes about 6 cups.

1/2 cup (1 stick) butter
1/2 cup (1 stick) margarine
2 cups sugar
4 eggs
2 cups flour
1 (5-ounce) can evaporated milk
1 teaspoon vanilla extract
Butterscotch Icing (below)

- CREAM THE BUTTER, margarine and sugar in a mixing bowl until fluffy. Add the eggs 1 at a time, beating well after each addition. Add the flour and milk alternately, beginning and ending with the flour. Stir in the vanilla. Spoon the batter into 2 greased and floured 9-inch round cake pans.

- Bake at 325 degrees for 20 to 30 minutes or until a wooden pick inserted in the center comes out clean. Let cake cool completely. Spread Butterscotch Icing between the layers and over the top and side of the cake.

Butterscotch Icing

MAKES ABOUT **4** CUPS

1 1/2 cups packed light brown sugar
3/4 cup (1 1/2 sticks) butter
1 1/2 teaspoons vanilla extract
1 1/2 cups sugar
3/4 cup milk

- COMBINE THE BROWN sugar, butter, vanilla, sugar and milk in a large saucepan. Bring to a rolling boil over medium-high heat. Boil until the mixture reaches 240 degrees on a candy thermometer, soft-ball stage. Remove from the heat and beat until the mixture is of a spreading consistency.

Lemon Curd Tartlets

MAKES **8** SERVINGS

Pecan Crust
1 cup (2 sticks) unsalted
   butter, softened
1/4 cup sugar
3/4 cup finely chopped
   pecans
1 egg
1 egg yolk
1 teaspoon salt
2 3/4 cups flour

Lemon Filling
1 cup (2 sticks) unsalted
   butter, melted
2 cups sugar
4 eggs
1 cup (scant) fresh lemon
   juice

Assembly
3/4 cup finely chopped
   pistachios
Whipped cream

• FOR THE CRUST, combine the butter, sugar, pecans, egg, egg yolk and salt in a large bowl, stirring with a wooden spoon just until blended. Add the flour and knead until a smooth ball forms. Wrap in plastic wrap. Chill for 4 hours.

• Roll dough to a 1/4-inch thickness. Cut to fit into 8 individual tart pans. Fit pastry into pans; crust will be thick. Bake at 350 degrees for 12 to 15 minutes or until edges begin to brown. Let cool.

• For the filling, combine the butter, sugar, eggs and lemon juice in the top of a double boiler over simmering water. Cook for 7 minutes or until mixture is pale yellow and thickly coats the back of a spoon, stirring constantly and gently so that no air is incorporated. Strain and cool.

• To assemble, remove the tartlet shells from the pans. Pour the lemon filling into the shells. Sprinkle with the pistachios. Serve with whipped cream.

Summer Fruit Tart

MAKES **8** SERVINGS

1 (2-crust) pie pastry
6 ounces cream cheese, softened
Sour cream
4 peaches or nectarines, peeled and sliced
Seedless grapes, halved
Blueberries
Strawberries, sliced
3/4 cup orange juice
2 tablespoons cornstarch
2 tablespoons sugar
1/4 teaspoon mace
1/2 cup currant jelly
Red food coloring

- PRESS THE PASTRY into a pizza pan, cutting to fit. Bake at 450 degrees until crust is golden brown. Let cool. Mix the cream cheese in a small bowl with enough sour cream to make it spreadable. Spread the mixture over the crust. Arrange the peaches around the outside edge of the crust. Fill the center with a mixture of grapes, blueberries and strawberries.

- Combine the orange juice, cornstarch, sugar, mace and currant jelly in a saucepan. Bring to a boil over medium heat, stirring frequently. Cook until the jelly is melted. Let cool. Stir in a few drops of red food coloring. Pour over the fruit.

Mississippi's Best Peach Pie

MAKES **6** SERVINGS

1 (unbaked) deep-dish pie shell
3 cups (about) quartered fresh peaches
1 cup sugar
2 tablespoons flour
2 eggs, lightly beaten
Juice of 1 lemon
1/2 teaspoon vanilla extract
1/4 cup (1/2 stick) butter, melted

- LINE THE PIE shell with the peaches. Combine the sugar, flour, eggs, lemon juice, vanilla and butter in a large bowl and mix well. Pour over the peaches.

- Bake at 325 degrees for 1 hour or until the filling is set in the center; test by gently shaking the pie.

Cookie Crust Fudge Pie

MAKES **8** SERVINGS

1 cup (2 sticks) butter,
   softened
1 cup sugar
1/4 cup baking cocoa
1/4 cup flour
2 eggs, beaten
1 teaspoon vanilla extract
1 teaspoon instant coffee
   granules
1 tablespoon coffee-flavor
   liqueur
Pinch of salt
1 cup chopped pecans
1 Oreo cookie pie shell

- COMBINE THE BUTTER, sugar, baking cocoa and flour in a large bowl and mix well. Add the eggs, vanilla, coffee granules, coffee liqueur, salt and pecans and mix well. Pour the mixture into the pie shell.

- Bake at 375 degrees for 25 to 30 minutes. Do not overbake; filling will not be firm in the center. Serve warm with ice cream or whipped cream.

Classic Pecan Pie

MAKES **6** SERVINGS

1/2 cup (1 stick) butter
3 eggs
1 cup dark corn syrup
1/2 cup sugar
1 teaspoon vanilla extract
1 unbaked (9-inch) pie shell
1 cup chopped pecans

- MELT THE BUTTER in a saucepan. Beat the eggs in a bowl. Add the butter to the eggs with the corn syrup, sugar and vanilla and mix well. Line the bottom of the pie shell with the pecans. Pour the butter mixture over the pecans. Place the pie dish on a baking sheet.

- Bake at 350 degrees for 8 minutes. Reduce the oven temperature to 300 degrees. Bake for 40 to 60 minutes longer or until the filling is set in the center.

Pumpkin Chiffon Pie

MAKES 8 SERVINGS

3 egg yolks
$1/2$ cup sugar
$1^1/4$ cups canned pumpkin
$1/2$ cup milk
$1/2$ teaspoon salt
$1/2$ teaspoon ginger
$1/2$ teaspoon nutmeg
$1/2$ teaspoon cinnamon
1 tablespoon gelatin
$1/4$ cup cold water
$1/2$ cup sugar
3 egg whites
1 baked (9-inch) pie shell

- BEAT THE EGG yolks slightly in the top of a double boiler. Add the $1/2$ cup sugar, pumpkin, milk, salt, ginger, nutmeg and cinnamon and mix well. Cook over simmering water until thickened, stirring frequently.

- Sprinkle the gelatin over the $1/4$ cup cold water in a cup. Let stand until softened. Add to the pumpkin mixture and mix well. Let cool. When the mixture begins to set, stir in the $1/2$ cup sugar.

- Beat the egg whites in a mixing bowl until soft peaks form. Fold into pumpkin mixture. Spoon the mixture into the pie shell. Refrigerate, covered, until firm. Garnish with whipped cream.

Chocolate Almond Puffs

1 (17-ounce) package puff pastry sheets, thawed
1 egg
1 to 2 tablespoons milk
9 to 18 Hershey's golden almond nuggets or about 6 ounces semisweet chocolate, cut into chunks
Sugar or brown sugar for sprinkling (optional)

- ROLL EACH PASTRY sheet to a 12-inch square on a lightly floured work surface. Cut each into 9 squares. Arrange the squares on a buttered or parchment-lined baking sheet.

- Whisk the egg and milk in a small bowl until frothy. Brush a small amount of the mixture on 2 adjacent sides of each square. Reserve remaining egg mixture.

- Divide the chocolate among the squares. Fold the pastry over to form a triangle, enclosing the chocolate. Press the edges with a fork to seal. Place the pastries on a baking sheet. Refrigerate, covered, until chilled.

- Just before baking brush the pastries with the remaining egg mixture. Sprinkle with sugar. Bake at 400 degrees for 15 to 20 minutes or until golden brown. Let cool for 10 minutes. Serve warm.

- NOTE: You may substitute confectioners' sugar for the sugar or brown sugar, sprinkling the pastries after removing them from the oven.

Chocolate Sherry Cream Bars

MAKES 25 SERVINGS

Chocolate Base

2 ounces unsweetened
  chocolate
1/2 cup (1 stick) unsalted
  butter
2 eggs
1 cup sugar
1/2 teaspoon vanilla extract
1/2 cup flour
1/4 teaspoon salt

Sherry Filling

2 cups confectioners' sugar
1/4 cup (1/2 stick) unsalted
  butter, softened
2 tablespoons heavy cream
2 tablespoons dry sherry
1/2 cup chopped walnuts or
  pecans

Chocolate Topping

1/2 cup chocolate chips
2 tablespoons water
2 tablespoons unsalted
  butter

- FOR THE BASE, melt the chocolate and butter in a small saucepan over low heat, stirring frequently. Let cool slightly. Beat the eggs in a large bowl. Add the sugar and beat until thickened and pale yellow. Stir in the chocolate mixture, vanilla, flour and salt.

- Grease and flour an 8x8-inch baking pan. Line with parchment paper or waxed paper. Spoon the batter into the prepared pan. Bake at 325 degrees for 25 to 30 minutes or until a tester inserted in the center comes out clean. Cool completely in the pan. Invert onto a plate. Remove paper.

- For the filling, beat the confectioners' sugar and butter in a mixing bowl. Add the cream and sherry and beat until smooth. Stir in the walnuts. Spread over the chocolate base. Chill, covered, until firm.

- For the topping, combine the chocolate chips, water and butter in a small saucepan. Cook over low heat until chocolate chips are melted, stirring constantly. Spread over the filling. Chill until the topping has hardened. Trim off crisp edges and cut into small bars.

Oatmeal Chiperoos

MAKES ABOUT **60** COOKIES

1 cup (2 sticks) butter, softened
3/4 cup packed brown sugar
3/4 cup sugar
2 eggs
2 teaspoons vanilla extract
1 1/2 cups flour
1 teaspoon baking soda
1 teaspoon salt
1 cup chopped pecans or walnuts
2 cups rolled oats
2 cups chocolate chips

- CREAM THE BUTTER, brown sugar and sugar in a mixing bowl until light and fluffy. Beat in the eggs and vanilla. Sift the flour with the baking soda and salt. Add to the butter mixture and mix well. Stir in pecans, oats and chocolate chips.

- Drop tablespoonfuls of the batter onto greased cookie sheets. Bake at 350 degrees for 12 to 15 minutes or until golden brown. Cool on wire racks.

Gingersnaps

MAKES **60** COOKIES

1 1/2 cups shortening
2 cups sugar
2 eggs
1/2 cup molasses
4 cups flour
1 tablespoon ginger
1 tablespoon cloves
1 tablespoon cinnamon
2 teaspoons baking soda
1/2 teaspoon salt
Sugar

- CREAM THE SHORTENING and 2 cups sugar in a mixing bowl until fluffy. Beat in the eggs and molasses. Sift the flour with the ginger, cloves, cinnamon, baking soda and salt. Stir into the shortening mixture until a soft dough forms.

- Roll small bits of dough into balls. Roll in sugar to coat. Arrange 1 1/2 inches apart on ungreased cookie sheets. Bake at 350 degrees for 10 minutes for chewy cookies, 12 to 13 minutes for crisp cookies. Cool on wire racks.

- NOTE: You may freeze baked cookies.

Pecan-Topped Drop Cookies

MAKES 24 COOKIES

1/2 cup (1 stick) butter,
  softened
1 cup sugar
1 egg
1 1/2 cups baking mix
1 teaspoon vanilla extract
24 pecan halves

- BEAT THE BUTTER and sugar in a mixing bowl until fluffy. Add the egg and beat well. Add the baking mix and beat well. Beat in the vanilla. Drop by spoonfuls onto a greased cookie sheet. Press a pecan half into the top of each cookie. Bake at 350 degrees for 6 minutes. Cool on wire racks.

Ranger Cookies

MAKES 180 COOKIES

1 cup shortening
1 cup packed brown sugar
1 cup sugar
2 eggs
2 cups flour
1 teaspoon baking soda
1/2 teaspoon baking powder
1 teaspoon salt
2 cups quick-cooking
  rolled oats
2 cups crisp rice cereal
1 cup shredded coconut
1 cup grated apples
1 teaspoon vanilla extract
2 tablespoons grated
  orange zest

- CREAM THE SHORTENING, brown sugar and sugar in a mixing bowl until fluffy. Beat in the eggs. Sift the flour with the baking soda, baking powder and salt. Add to the sugar mixture and mix well. Stir in the oats, cereal, coconut, apples, vanilla and orange zest.

- Drop by teaspoonfuls onto greased cookie sheets. Bake at 375 degrees for 11 minutes. Cool on wire racks.

Bananas Foster

6 bananas
3/4 cup (1 1/2 sticks) butter
1 1/2 cups packed dark
   brown sugar
1 1/2 teaspoons cinnamon
2 ounces banana liqueur
1 cup dark rum, warmed
1 quart French vanilla ice
   cream

- CUT THE BANANAS into halves lengthwise and quarter. Melt the butter with the brown sugar and cinnamon in a flat-bottomed skillet over low heat, stirring to mix well. Add the banana liqueur and mix well. Add the bananas and stir gently to coat.

- Add the rum and carefully ignite with a long match. Baste the bananas with the sauce until the flames die down. Serve the bananas over the ice cream.

Blueberry Crisp

MAKES **8** SERVINGS

4 cups fresh blueberries
1/2 cup (1 stick) butter,
   melted
1 cup flour
1 cup packed brown sugar
1/4 cup rolled oats

- SPOON THE BLUEBERRIES into a greased 1- to 1 1/2-quart baking dish. Combine the butter, flour, brown sugar and oats in a large bowl and mix well. Crumble the mixture over the blueberries, covering the blueberries evenly.

- Bake at 350 degrees for 30 minutes. Serve warm with ice cream.

For **Raspberry Sauce,** combine 3 to 4 pints raspberries with 3 tablespoons water in a blender container. Process on "grind" or "frappé" until berries are liquified. Blend in 3 tablespoons confectioners' sugar and 1 tablespoon orange-flavor liqueur.

Pour the berry mixture through a fine sieve, straining out the seeds. Discard the seeds and bulky pieces of pulp. Spoon the sauce into a serving bowl. Refrigerate, covered, until chilled. Serve with vanilla ice cream. You may also make this sauce from fresh strawberries. May store in an airtight container in the freezer.

Poached Pears

MAKES **6** SERVINGS

2¹/₂ pounds ripe pears
2 cups dry white wine
¹/₂ cup sugar
Julienned peel of 1 lemon
1 (2-inch) cinnamon stick, or
   ¹/₄ teaspoon cinnamon
1 (1-inch) piece vanilla
   bean, or 1 teaspoon
   vanilla extract
¹/₄ cup orange marmalade
¹/₄ cup apricot preserves

- PEEL THE PEARS and cut into eighths, discarding the core. Combine the pears, wine and sugar in a saucepan. Add the lemon peel to the saucepan. Bring the mixture to a boil over medium heat.

- Simmer for 5 to 10 minutes or until the pears are tender. Transfer the pears and lemon peel to a serving dish. Bring the liquid in the saucepan to a boil. Add the cinnamon stick, vanilla bean, marmalade and preserves. Cook for 10 minutes; discard cinnamon stick and vanilla bean. Pour over the pears. Chill, covered, until ready to serve.

Lemon Ice Cream

MAKES **2 ¹/₂** QUARTS

2 cups sugar
1 cup lemon juice
1 quart light cream or
   half-and-half
1 quart milk
8 teaspoons grated lemon
   zest
Few drops of yellow food
   coloring

- COMBINE THE SUGAR and lemon juice in a large bowl and mix well. Add the cream and mix well. Add the milk, lemon zest and food coloring and mix well. Pour into an ice cream freezer container. Freeze according to manufacturer's directions.

- NOTE: Serve with Raspberry Sauce (at left).

Peachy Plum Ice Cream

MAKES ABOUT 1 ½ QUARTS

1½ cups milk
2 cups sugar
Dash of salt
1½ cups half-and-half
2½ cups heavy cream
1½ teaspoons vanilla
   extract
3 cups puréed peaches
1½ cups puréed plums

- HEAT THE MILK in a large saucepan over medium-high heat until bubbles form around the edge, stirring constantly. Remove from the heat. Add the sugar and salt, stirring until dissolved. Add the half-and-half, heavy cream and vanilla and mix well.

- Refrigerate, covered, for 30 minutes. Add the peaches and plums and mix well. Pour into an ice cream freezer container. Freeze according to manufacturer's directions.

Mint Sherbet

MAKES 8 SERVINGS

1 cup milk
½ cup fresh mint leaves,
   finely chopped
¾ cup sugar
¼ cup light corn syrup
1 cup half-and-half
1 cup drained crushed
   pineapple
Lemon juice to taste
Few drops of green food
   coloring

- HEAT THE MILK in a small saucepan over medium-high heat until bubbles form around the edge, stirring constantly. Place the mint in a bowl and pour the milk over it. Let stand for 1 hour. Strain, discarding the mint. Combine the milk with the sugar, corn syrup, half-and-half, pineapple, lemon juice and food coloring in a large bowl, stirring until sugar dissolves.

- Pour the mixture into a rigid plastic container and place in the freezer. Freeze, covered, for 3 hours. Beat the mixture with a fork to break up the ice crystals. Freeze, covered, until firm.

Toffee Crunch

MAKES ABOUT 16 SERVINGS

1 (16-ounce) package
  ladyfingers
1 quart chocolate almond
  ice cream, softened
6 to 8 chocolate-covered
  toffee bars, crushed
1 quart coffee ice cream,
  softened
1 cup whipping cream
2 tablespoons sugar

- SPLIT THE LADYFINGERS into halves lengthwise. Line the bottom and side of a 9- or 10-inch springform pan with the ladyfingers. Spoon the chocolate almond ice cream onto the ladyfingers, spreading evenly. Top with the crushed toffee bars.

- Spoon the coffee ice cream over the candy, spreading evenly. Freeze, covered, until firm.

- Whip the cream in a chilled bowl with chilled beaters until soft peaks form. Add the sugar gradually, whipping until stiff peaks form.

- Remove the side of the springform pan. Frost the dessert with the whipped cream. To serve, cut into slices or remove with an ice cream scoop.

Ice Glacé Pie

Chocolate Crust

1/2 (11-ounce) package pie
   crust mix
3/4 cup walnuts, chopped
1/4 cup packed brown sugar
1 ounce unsweetened
   chocolate, grated
2 tablespoons water
1 teaspoon vanilla extract

Ice Cream Filling

1 quart chocolate or
   chocolate fudge ice
   cream, softened
1 quart English toffee, coffee
   nut or coffee ice cream,
   softened

Coffee Whipped Cream

1 cup whipping cream
2 tablespoons confectioners'
   sugar
2 teaspoons instant coffee
   granules

- FOR THE CRUST, combine the pie crust mix, walnuts, brown sugar and chocolate in a medium bowl and mix with a fork. Add the water and vanilla and mix well. Press the mixture over the bottom and up the side of a greased 9-inch pie dish, using moistened hands. Bake at 375 degrees for 20 minutes. Cool slightly. Freeze, covered, for at least 1 hour before filling

- For the filling, spoon the chocolate ice cream into the crust until half full, spreading evenly. Spoon English toffee ice cream into the shell until full, spreading evenly. Freeze, covered, for at least 2 hours.

- For the whipped cream, whip the cream with the confectioners' sugar and coffee granules in a mixing bowl until stiff peaks form. Spoon over the ice cream, making swirls, or pipe through a pastry bag fitted with a #6 rosette tip. Store, covered, in the freezer until ready to serve.

- To serve, let stand at room temperature for 5 to 10 minutes before slicing. Garnish with chocolate curls.

Recipe Contributors

Jen Acree
Virginia Adair
Polly Adams
Bonnie Adler
Louise Allen
Gayle Alston
John G. Alston, Jr.
Jean Astrop
Jeane Austin
Robyn Barkin
Sherrie Bianco
Octavia Birnie
Sally Bland
Virginia Blandford
Fay Brewer
Nancy Carithers
Alice Carr
Anne Carr
Le Carr
Jill Carroll
Nancy Caswell
Cathy Christians
Charles Clark
Jacqueline Clark
Bunny Clarke
Judi Clifford
Peggy Clinkscales
Muffet Corse
Charles Crawford
Susan Croft
Louise Cronan
David Curry
Anne Curtis
Carol Curtis

Caroline Davis
June Davis
Bobi Dimond
J. Michael Driver
Barbara Dulin
Betty Edge
Dorothy Fuqua
Duvall Fuqua
Marcia Gaddis
Martha Garlington
Ken Gearon
Olguita Goizueta
Carol Goodman
Carole Graves
Nancy Green
Barbara Griffin
Elizabeth Hale
Carol Hall
Wynn C. Henderson
Wynn H. Henderson
Wanda Hopkins
Fay Howell
Robin Howell
Katie Hutchison
Margaret Hutchison
Kerry Izard
Helen Justice
Ginger Kennedy
Anne Preston King
Bradley Kirsch
Pat Krebs
Robin Lea
Mrs. Leonard Long
Joyce and Henri Loustau

Nancy Lynn
Christienne MacKaye
Bettye Maddox
Danny Marentette
Cookie McClendon
Cindy Mills
Rhonda Milner
Mary Mobley
Gwyneth Moran
Wesley Moran
Betty Mullen
Rene Nalley
Kevin Naylor
Jennifer Nichols
Jo Ann Nicholson
Mary Juliet Nicholson
Mary and Felton
    Norwood
Betty Nunnally
Jean Nunnally
Helen Olnick
Peaches Page
Joan Pattillo
Sarah English
    Perry
Marnie Porson
Caroline Powell
Ethel Prescott
Betsy Pritchett
Eleanor Ratchford
Sue Ratliff
Alice Richards
Helen Rieser
Julie Robertson

Mary Rooker
Mary Scott Rooker
Marcy Sands
Peggy Schwall
Harriet Shaffer
Janet Shepherd
Anne Siebert
Becky Smith
Helen M. Smith
Laura M. Smith
Laura Spearman
Wanda Staebell
Dorothy Stribling
Lisa Sullivan
Carmen Talley
Margaretta Taylor
Pat Thomas
Gloria Thornwell
Betty Tucker
Susan Tucker
Jean Underwood
Carolyn Vigtel
Rosemary Walker
Becky Warner
Ruthie Watts
Betsy West
Jane Wheeler
Susan Wilcox
Sallie Wilgus
Loraine Williams
Marcellene Wilson
Marion Wright
Sissie Wright
Kathy York

Recipe Testers

Jen Acree
Bonnie Adler
Peggy Allen
Gayle Alston
Boyce Ansley
Jean Astrop
Robyn Barkin
Laura Blackburn
Virginia Bondurant
Jeanne Bowden
Jean Caldwell
Brandon Candler
Shannon Candler
Nancy Carithers
Le Carr
Nancy Caswell
Cathy Christians
Jacqueline Clark
Peggy Clinkscales
Flossie Collins
Martha Crabtree
Susan Croft
Louise Cronan
Anne Curtis
Carol Curtis
June Davis

Nora Ann Davis
J. Michael Driver
Barbara Dulin
Barbara Eddins
Susan Faulk
Ken Gearon
Rebecca Wayne
    Gibson
Carol Goodman
Bev Green
Nancy Green
Becky Guberman
Elizabeth Hale
Abbie Harlin
Ann Harrison
Wynn H. Henderson
Lynne Holley
Nancy Hooff
Wanda Hopkins
Robin Howell
Linda Hull
Margaret Hutchison
Jane Lanier
Robin Lea
Jennifer Lee
Cappy Livezey

Gray Lynn
Nancy Lynn
Bettye Maddox
Mary Ann Massey
Marianne McConnel
Betsy McDonald
Marjette McDonnell
Cindy Mills
Rhonda Milner
Mary Mobley
Wesley Moran
Rene Nalley
Jo Ann Nicholson
Mary and Felton
    Norwood
Jean Nunnally
Sally Nunnally
Peaches Page
Sallie Patterson
Bet Pope
Lou Post
Ethel Prescott
Barbara Prickett
Betsy Pritchett
Perry Raulet
Joyce Rees

Helen Rieser
Julie Robertson
Marcia Robinson
Cindy Rooker
Mary Scott Rooker
Harriet Shaffer
Becky Smith
Dean Smith
Sophie Smulders
Laura Spearman
Lisa Sullivan
Carmen Talley
Pat Thomas
Susan Tucker
Judy Varn
Carolyn Vigtel
Becky Warner
Harriet Warren
Ginger Watkins
Jody Weatherly
Betsy West
Jane Wheeler
Sharon Wiggins
Nancy Willcoxon
Kathy York
Camille Yow

Index

Index

Index

Index

Index

Index

The Swan's Palette

A collection of recipes from
the Forward Arts Foundation

3130 Slaton Drive, Northwest
Atlanta, Georgia 30305
404-261-9855
www.swancoachhouse.com